Embracing the
Divine Feminine

Embracing the Divine Feminine

Finding God through the Ecstasy of Physical Love— The Song of Songs Annotated & Explained

Translation & Annotation by Rabbi Rami Shapiro

Foreword by Rev. Cynthia Bourgeault, PhD

For People of All Faiths, All Backgrounds
JEWISH LIGHTS Publishing
Woodstock, Vermont

Walking Together, Finding the Way ®
SKYLIGHT PATHS®
PUBLISHING
Woodstock, Vermont

Embracing the Divine Feminine:
Finding God through the Ecstasy of Physical Love—
The Song of Songs Annotated & Explained

2014 Quality Paperback Edition, First Printing
Translation, annotation, and introductory material © 2014 by Rami Shapiro
Foreword © 2014 by Cynthia Bourgeault

For information regarding permission to reprint material from this book, please mail or fax your request in writing to SkyLight Paths Publishing, Permissions Department, at the address / fax number listed below, or email your request to permissions@skylightpaths.com.

Library of Congress Cataloging-in-Publication Data
Embracing the divine feminine : finding God through the ecstasy of physical love : the Song of Songs annotated & explained / translation & annotation by Rabbi Rami Shapiro ; foreword by Rev. Cynthia Bourgeault, PhD.
    pages cm. — (Skylight illuminations series)
Includes bibliographical references and index.
ISBN 978-1-59473-575-2 (alk. paper) — ISBN 978-1-59473-592-9 (ebook : alk. paper)
1. Bible. Song of Solomon—Criticism, interpretation, etc. I. Shapiro, Rami M., annotator. II. Bible. Song of Solomon. English. Shapiro. 2014.
BS1485.52.E43 2014
223′.9077—dc23
                                        2014034636

10 9 8 7 6 5 4 3 2 1

Manufactured in the United States of America
Cover design: Walter C. Bumford, III, Stockton, Massachusetts, and Jenny Buono
Cover art: © bruniewska/Shutterstock

SkyLight Paths, "Walking Together, Finding the Way" and colophon are trademarks of LongHill Partners, Inc., registered in the U.S. Patent and Trademark Office.

Walking Together, Finding the Way
Published by SkyLight Paths Publishing/Jewish Lights Publishing
Divisions of LongHill Partners, Inc.
Sunset Farm Offices, Route 4, P.O. Box 237
Woodstock, VT 05091
Tel: (802) 457-4000   Fax: (802) 457-4004
www.skylightpaths.com   www.jewishlights.com

To my sister, Debbie, whose strength and compassion are a blessing to all who know her and benefit from her undying love.

And to my rebbe, Rabbi Zalman Schachter-Shalomi (z"l), who with his passing proves daily that "love is as strong as death."

Contents ☐

Foreword ☐

Cynthia Bourgeault

The Song of Songs is full of surprises, but first and foremost among these must certainly be the surprise that it made it into sacred scripture in the first place. Whatever genres of spiritual instruction would normally be deemed appropriate for inclusion in the sacred canon (the Five Books of Moses, the Prophets, and Writings in the case of the Hebrew scriptures), certainly erotica is not one of them. But biblical erotica is exactly what the Song is; there is no way around that fact once you allow yourself to see it. In perhaps the longest-running "the emperor has no clothes on" double take in spiritual history, generation upon generation of spiritual seekers have pushed beyond their pious preconceptions to discover, leaping off the pages right before their eyes, one of the most unabashedly sensuous, outrageous, and delicious celebrations of human erotic pleasuring ever to have seen the light of day. What gives?

Part of the reason, of course, for the Song's inclusion among the wisdom writings of the Hebrew scriptures is its traditional association with King Solomon. (In Protestant versions of the Bible, the Song is in fact titled the "Song of Solomon.") Given Solomon's legendary reputation for wisdom and his long, resplendent reign at the pinnacle of Israel's glory, it would be pretty much guaranteed that anything bearing his name would have a certain immunity within the sacred canon, no matter what its content. And, of course, as Rabbi Rami explains in this book, the Song passed under the radar screen because it was so quickly allegorized, first by Judaism and then by Christianity, where the Song was seen, respectively, as an elaborate metaphor for God's love for Israel or God's love for the church. As long as we all agree that breasts are not really breasts and copulation is not really copulation, it all works out just fine. That is exactly how the Song has been interpreted for the better part of its long history by a distinguished cast of pious rabbis and celibate monks.

Yet, it's not a matter of simply pulling the wool over the eyes of gullible old holy men. When the celebrated Rabbi Akiva states unequivocally in the early second century CE that "all scripture is holy, but the Song of Songs is the Holy of Holies" (*Mishnah Yadayim* 3:5), he is responding to something more than either allegorical naiveté or unconscious libido. The mysterious secret of the Song is that in spite of all efforts to dress it up or dress it down, disguise it, or transfigure it beyond recognition, something remains that is so crystal clear, transparent, universal, and compelling that it goes straight to the mystical bull's-eye of the heart. Allegorizing it does not blunt this edge, nor does acknowledging the blatant eroticism degrade it. The Song sings, in its own voice, of something so universally true and spiritually luminous that it eventually wins over all but the most puritanically repressed to its own elusive charm.

That element, as I would see it, is the transfiguring power of love. I mean this in two ways: love as it transfigures those who engage with it, and love as it itself is transfigured by its noblest players—those who are not merely lovers but *lovers of truth*, from myopically narcissistic desiring into something approaching luminous wisdom. The Song has no plot, so to speak; its two lovers simply play "hide and seek" through eight successive, almost surrealistic freeze frames. Yet, something happens, and the spiritually attuned heart picks up on it. Somewhere between chapter 2 and chapter 3 the male lover goes missing, and the woman, with wrenching determination, confirms her fidelity to her beloved and to the path of love: "I will leave my bed and wander the city, searching street and square for you for whom my breath pants" (Song of Songs 3:2).

Reunion, consummation, erotic bliss hurtle by, again in the Song's allusive, freeze-frame way, and then at the beginning of chapter 6 another separation allusively looms, along with hints of rejection by society and family members. Another reunion and, finally, out of the blue, comes that impassioned affirmation that is no doubt among the top ten of the most stirring and luminous proclamations ever uttered in all of literature:

> Set me as a seal upon your heart,
> as an insignia upon your arm;
> for love is strong as death,
> passion as fierce as the grave;
> its smallest spark is a flash of fire
> igniting an inferno.
>
> (SONG 8:6)

All of a sudden things have jumped from the launchpad of erotica to land in the domain of mystical union, with this soul-stirring proclamation of the ultimate dominion of love, the ultimate certainty of an alchemical fusion of souls that exceeds all space and time, all human loss and bereavement. How did we get here?

As I said, the Song is full of surprises. There is a freshness—just as in love itself—that makes all things new.

During its long, singular career as the beloved black sheep in the fold of sacred scripture, the Song has gone through many interpretive fashions. As mentioned already, for the better part of its interpretive history its light has been filtered through a thick allegorical fogbank, in which its explicitly sexual reference points were sublimated and obscured. Not surprisingly, that tendency has now fallen victim to the naturalistic temperament of postmodern times, and at this point the pendulum seems to have swung decisively toward celebrating the Song as, variously, a social critique, an early feminist document, and, above all, an unabashedly explicit celebration of sensuality, amorality, and the life of the body.

This is perhaps a necessary corrective to the former generations of allegorical excess. But it too leaves something out. If the former approach erred, too, heavily on the side of obfuscating the erotic current running through the Song, the present generation errs on the side of missing the profoundly mysterious and spiritual current that saturates the Song, not in spite of its eroticism but because of it and through it.

In this sparkling new translation, Rabbi Rami swings the interpretive pendulum back toward the allegorical—but with a distinct difference. If a former mode of allegorical interpretation insisted on disguising and blunting the erotic passion that is the Song's native tongue, Rami insists on bringing the eroticism fully into sight and celebrating it as the primary thrust of the Song's transformative trajectory. In his highly imaginative and yet scholarly reading, the affair between the woman and her beloved becomes an elaborate allegory for Lady Wisdom and all authentic seekers of Wisdom (in other words, *you!*). The journey by which raw eros moves toward luminous Wisdom is, not surprisingly, the same journey traveled by the Song's anonymous lovers. The journey that all seekers of Wisdom will ultimately traverse in the cave of their own heart's erotic desire is slowly transformed into luminous agape through mutual caring, fidelity, and surrender to the path itself.

The analogy Rabbi Rami sets before us is profound, doing no violence to the naturalistic reading of the Song, while evoking its mysterious transformative power in a universal and highly accessible new context. He also, in a wonderful and perhaps unintended way, brings the interpretive history of the Song full circle by returning it definitively to the domain of wisdom literature, showing us clearly why the Song does in fact belong in sacred scripture and why sacred scripture would not be even remotely so sacred without it. In the spirit of our own age, Rabbi Rami reaffirms the ancient truth that true lovers—both of God and of each other—have always known: that eros can never be separated from divine creative love, for the two are ultimately joined at the hip. And the path to Wisdom travels, inescapably, through love's purifying flames.

Enjoy this beautiful new translation and the Song of Song's ever-surprising freshness, all the more highlighted in these stunning new literary vestments.

Acknowledgments ☐

This book owes its birth to Cynthia Bourgeault and her book *The Meaning of Mary Magdalene*, in which she speaks of Lady Wisdom and the Song of Songs in the context of the Gospels. One day in a brief telephone conversation, Cynthia suggested that we collaborate on a Song of Songs weekend retreat. While unclear as to what I had to offer in this regard, I am loath to miss out on any opportunity to teach with and learn from Cynthia, so I agreed.

Faced with three days of retreat to fill with meaningful insights into the Song of Songs, I delved into the Song and her many commentaries, and after several months I suspected that a book was emerging from my notes. The Song began to speak to me in ways not previously seen in the commentaries I was reading—ways that I felt could, if shared, be of benefit to larger numbers of people than a weekend retreat could accommodate.

As I usually do when I find myself deeply immersed in translating and commenting on the Hebrew Bible, I contacted Emily Wichland at SkyLight Paths and sent her my notes to see if she, too, thought there was a book emerging from them. She did, and thus began our twelfth collaboration.

My thanks to Cynthia for suggesting the topic, to Emily for polishing my rough draft, and to all the great people at SkyLight Paths for believing in this project and bringing this book to market. As always, it is a pleasure working with you all.

The Song of Songs
as the Holy of Holies

Singing the Song of Songs may be hazardous to your spiritual well-being. This, at least, is the opinion of the first-century sage Rabbi Akiva ben Joseph. According to Rabbi Akiva, treating the Song of Songs as an erotic love poem and singing it in bars or at parties will cost you your place in the world to come.[1] While I don't encourage singing the Song in bars, I do encourage you to read it as an erotic love poem.

Even if you don't worry much about the afterlife, there is still reason enough to beware the Song. Another Talmudic sage, whose name was not preserved but who seems to be in line with Akiva's thinking, argues that to treat the Song of Songs as a song is to bring grave evil into the world.[2] This, too, isn't something with which I am overly concerned. There is more than enough evil in the world, and I doubt this love song will add anything to it. In fact, reading the Song of Songs the way we shall read it here may actually lessen some of that evil.

Defiling the Hands

The problem the ancient sages had with the Song of Songs was not with the Song itself. On the contrary, the same Rabbi Akiva who was so incensed about singing the Song at parties was convinced that the Song of Songs was the heart of God's revelation to Israel and hence "defiled the hands."

"Defiling the hands" (mitamin et hayadayim) is a Rabbinic euphemism assigned to books that are considered holy. In the days of the early Rabbis, texts were written on parchment scrolls and stored loosely in what we today might call a library's stacks. The sages would often study these texts while eating, and crumbs would get rolled up with the scrolls when the scrolls were returned to the stacks, attracting hungry mice to munch on the scrolls in hopes of finding a treat. To keep the scrolls from being eaten, the sages had to find a way to prevent their colleagues from snacking while reading them. Their solution was to declare the scrolls holy and to rule that touching holy scrolls put one's hands in a state of spiritual purity that made their use in such mundane activities as eating inappropriate. Declaring that a specific book "defiled the hands" was a way of declaring it holy.

When it came to the Song of Songs and the book of Ecclesiastes, two texts that along with the book of Proverbs were thought to be authored by King Solomon,[3] the Rabbis differed as to whether these books defiled the hands.

The argument recorded in the Talmud wasn't about whether the Song of Songs or the book of Ecclesiastes should be included in the Hebrew canon—they were already listed as such in the Talmud[4]—but whether they should have been included.

Rabbi Judah complained that while the Song of Songs certainly defiled the hands, Ecclesiastes did not. His contemporary Rabbi Jose had doubts about both books. That was when Rabbi Akiva jumped into the argument to defend the Song, if not Ecclesiastes:

> How dare you say such a thing! No one has ever argued against the Song of Songs defiling one's hands! The entire universe is not as worthy as the single day on which the Song of Songs was given to Israel. The entire scripture is holy, and the Song of Songs is the Holy of Holies![5]

Given its stature as the Holy of Holies, it is not surprising to find Akiva bemoaning the Song being sung at parties and threatening to bar those who did so from heaven. But what is it about this blatantly erotic love poem that made it the Holy of Holies?

The answer is not in the Song itself but in the allegorical interpretation read into it. While on the surface the Song of Songs is a love poem between a woman and a man, in the hands of Rabbinic and later church interpreters, the Song became a celebration of God's love for his beloved Israel—for the Rabbis—and Christ's love for his beloved church—for Christian commentators. It is their interpretation of the Song of Songs that rabbis like Akiva seek to protect, and not the Song per se.

Who Wrote the Song of Songs and When?

The opening verse of the Song of Songs—"The Song of Songs, by Solomon"—implies that the Song was written by the tenth-century-BCE Israelite monarch King Solomon. This is almost certainly an act of pseudepigrapha, Greek for "false ascription." To gain legitimacy and readership for their books, ancient writers would often ascribe their work to a more famous and long-dead person. In the case of the Song of Songs, this person is King Solomon.

To bolster the Song's claim of Solomonic authorship, some scholars point to references of wealth scattered throughout the Song. For example, the woman central to the Song appears independently wealthy. She has her own vineyard (1:6), herds of sheep (1.8), and a house of cedar and pine (1:17); she sleeps in her own bed in her own room decorated with latticework (2:9); she wears shoes (7:2) and washes her feet before going to sleep (5:3); she wears jewelry (1:10) and a veil (4:1) and employs a wide variety of expensive spices and oils (1:12–14, 3:6, 5:5). Such wealth, they say, suggests that this woman is a member of King Solomon's court.

While it is true that the woman in the Song appears wealthy and displays an extraordinary amount of social independence, there is no reason why this should link her or the Song to Solomon. Even overt mentions of the king himself fail to do that (1:5, 3:7). We are dealing with a work of poetic imagination, and there is no reason to assume that a poet centuries removed from Solomon could not have imagined what the glory of the Solomonic age might have been like.

While internal references to wealth and King Solomon don't help us determine when the Song was written, the Hebrew the author employs might. The renowned Hebrew scholar H. L. Ginsberg dated the Hebrew of the Song of Songs to the third century BCE but left open the possibility that the text we have is not the original. Indeed, Rabbi Akiva's objection to singing the Song of Songs at parties suggests that the Song was committed to memory long before it was committed to parchment, and the written form may reflect a later form of Hebrew than the supposed oral original. In fact the written Song contains some Aramaic words, and Aramaic entered into the Hebrew language at the close of the sixth century BCE, so the Song may well predate its third-century-BCE written form by centuries. But even if one dates the Song of Songs to the sixth century BCE, that is still hundreds of years after the tenth-century-BCE reign of King Solomon.

The best one can do with dating the Song of Songs is to say that scholars differ and their differences range over an eight-hundred-year period from the tenth to the second century BCE. Luckily, not knowing the true author and exact date of the Song of Songs has no bearing on finding meaning in the Song itself.

Just an Old-Fashioned Love Song

Regardless of who wrote the Song of Songs and when, there is no doubt that it is a love song, a poem exploring the extreme sexual passion between an unnamed woman and her unnamed lover. Some see the Song as a collection of discrete love songs, and others as a single narrative poem covering a period of time in the lives of the lovers who are its protagonists. Moved by the work of Bar-Ilan Bible scholar Elie Assis, I fall somewhere in between:

The Song of Songs is not a collection of separate poems, but neither is it a plot-based narrative telling the story of a pair of lovers.
The Song of Songs is a unitary literary work, which has a beginning, a middle, and an end. The book is a single organism, and
if any of the individual poems were lacking, it would be incom-
plete. The order of the poems is also essential to its understanding. There are close affinities between many poems in the book,
which have a common vocabulary, common motifs, metaphors
and similes, moods and a common attitude towards the issue of
love. The innuendos and ambiguities, which are common in all
the poems, are crucial to the love poetry of the book.[6]

I would go a step further; perhaps a huge step further. While agreeing
with Assis that the innuendos of the Song are crucial to understanding it,
I would also say that the innuendos speak not simply to the erotic nature
of the lovers' encounters, but to the erotic nature of our meeting with
Lady Wisdom.

I am reading the Song of Songs as a fully sexualized allegory of love
between Wisdom and the seeker of Wisdom, a celebration of the psycho-
sexual-spiritual awakening to the unity of God, woman, man, and nature
that happens when a seeker of Wisdom embraces and is embraced by
Wisdom herself. As such, the sexual union at the heart of the Song is
vitally important.

Sexual love is the most intense and dramatic of the common
ways in which a human being comes into union and conscious
relationship with something outside himself. It is, furthermore,
the most vivid of man's customary expressions of his organic
spontaneity, the most positive and creative occasion of his being
transported by something beyond his conscious will.[7]

This "something" beyond our conscious will is God manifesting as God's
firstborn, Chochmah (Wisdom), Lady Wisdom, who reveals herself to us
in the book of Proverbs, and whom I take to be synonymous with the

Woman of Wholeness and Peace of the Song of Songs. Wisdom is not separate from creation; indeed, she is the way of creativity and the resulting creation. In Proverbs, Wisdom delights in humanity, calls to us, shares a meal with us (8:22–9:6), and in the Song of Songs, a bed as well. To know Wisdom, to receive the knowing that is Wisdom, one has to love Wisdom. As the unknown author of the fourteenth-century *Cloud of Unknowing* teaches us, "God can be grasped by love but never by concepts."[8]

There is nothing theoretical or abstract in the Song of Songs. The message is one of loving relationship, because the revelation is that all things are related. The Song of Songs uses the sexual to reach the spiritual and in this way reveals what Thomas Moore calls the "soul of sex."

> To appreciate the soul of sex, we may have to accomplish several things rather foreign to our current tastes and values. First, we have to learn how to enter the realm of the senses with abandon and trust, giving up our need to understand as we go down into sensation. Second, we have to discover the nature, workings, and validity of mystical experience, an equally difficult task in a culture that believes only in the existence of that which it can measure and prove. Third, and perhaps most difficult of all, we have to appreciate that these two tasks are inseparable, two sides of a coin, each a prerequisite for the other.[9]

I believe the Song of Songs does all three and, in doing so, shows reality to be a network of interdependent relationships rather than a collection of independent things. Here is how Jesus put this: "When you make the two into one, and when you make the inner like the outer and the outer like the inner, and the upper like the lower, and when you make male and female into a single one, so that the male will not be male nor the female be female … then you will enter [the kingdom]."[10] The "kingdom of heaven" isn't an otherworldly realm, but our earthly realm when viewed through the lens of love. The Song of Songs invites us to experience this love, to realize this unity, and to awaken to the kingdom of God within and around us.

The unification of opposites of which Jesus speaks and in which the Song of Song revels is not limited to the union of male and female and includes the union of human and nature as well. Both the woman and the man in the Song are compared to objects of the natural world: her breasts are like two fawns (4:5), his strength is like a cedar of Lebanon (5:15). There is no separation between humanity and nature; the human, as the Hebrew word *adam* (earthling) reminds us, is of the earth (*adamah*): human from humus. The unity the Song celebrates and to which it draws us is a fully embodied realization of the unity of God, woman, man, and nature:

> An organic natural order has its proper correspondence in a mode of consciousness which is a total feeling or experiencing. Where feeling is broken up into the feeler and the feeling, the knower and the known, what lies between the two is not relationship but mere juxtaposition.[11]

Our reading of the Song of Songs will focus on the awakening of the lover—the human seeker of Wisdom—to this "total feeling" of the unitive reality that Wisdom reveals.

Too Sexy for This Book

The Song of Songs uses the imagery of physical love and sexual union to express the "total feeling" that is spiritual awakening. For many commentators, the Song's explicit or lightly veiled sexuality is upsetting, and to avoid having to face it, they create allegorical masks behind which to hide the Song's freewheeling celebration of sexual love.

For example, so strong is their urge to avoid the sexuality of the Song of Songs that the editors of the ArtScroll *Tanach* (Hebrew scriptures) refuse to include a literal reading of the Song of Songs in their otherwise highly literal English translation of the Hebrew Bible. Citing the fact that commentators have read the Song allegorically for centuries, the ArtScroll introduction to the Song of Songs explains:

In the interest of accuracy, our translation of the Song is different from that of any other ArtScroll translation of Scripture.
Although we provide the literal meaning as part of the commentary, we translate the Song according to Rashi's allegorical
translation.[12]

We'll come to Rashi in a moment, but first let's deal with this notion that
not translating the Song of Songs literally is somehow in the interest of
accuracy. In essence the ArtScroll editors are saying, "In the interest of
accuracy we will not translate this text accurately." Or, "In the interest
of telling you what the Song of Songs means, we will not tell you what
the Song of Songs says."

Claiming that allegory equals accuracy is admitting that the text itself
as it has come down to us over the past twenty-two hundred years or
more cannot be trusted to convey the meaning the translators and commentators want it to convey. The Song is an erotic love poem featuring a
beautiful woman and her lover. While the poet uses a number of euphemisms for a variety of body parts and sexual acts, these are so thinly
veiled that only the thickest of allegorical overlays can even pretend to
mask them. Yet, this doesn't stop the Rabbis from trying.

In Song of Songs 7:3, for example, the male lover marvels at the
"navel" of his beloved, saying it is like "a rounded bowl never lacking
nectar." The poet is most likely referring to the woman's vagina wet with
desire. In the imagination of the Rabbis, however, this meaning is unten-
able, and something far different must be imposed on the text:

Rabbi Aha Haninah said: Scripture states, "Your navel is like a
rounded bowl wherein no nectar is wanting." *Your navel* refers
to the Sanhedrin [the rabbinic court]. How so? Just as the navel
is the center of the body, so the Sanhedrin is the center of the
world. Why a bowl? Just as a bowl protects the nectar it holds,
so the Sanhedrin protects the whole world. Why *round*? Just as
a bowl is moon-shaped, so we sit in a half-circle. And why *never*

lacking for nectar? Because the Sanhedrin is never wanting for a quorum of sages.[13]

I can't help but laugh when I read this. But I'm not laughing *at* my Rabbis but *with* them. The wording of the Song of Songs is not that subtle, and the ancient Rabbis certainly knew what the poet meant, and they knew that what he meant had nothing to do with the Sanhedrin, which in fact didn't even exist at the time the Song of Songs was composed. The great lengths to which the Rabbis go to make the Song say what it clearly does not and cannot say speaks to their love of this poem, even as it speaks to their discomfort with its plain meaning.

Long after Rabbi Aha's allegorical reading of the Song of Songs as a celebration of the Sanhedrin, Rabbi Shlomo Itzhaki (1040–1105), better known by the acronym RaSHI, read the Song of Songs through the lens of the Hebrew prophets who often used the analogy of loyal husband and disloyal wife when speaking of the relationship between God and the people Israel. According to Rashi:

Solomon composed the Song of Songs in the form of that same allegory. It is a passionate dialogue between the husband [God] who still loves his estranged exiled wife [Israel], who longs for her husband and seeks to endear herself to him again, as she recalls her youthful love for him and admits her guilt.[14]

The absurdity of Rashi's claim should be clear to anyone who reads the actual Song. First, the woman and man featured in the Song are not married, at least not to each other. Second, the woman neither expresses nor feels any shame or guilt. Third, there is no sense of estrangement between the lovers in the Song of Songs. While it is true that they are at times separated, they are not alienated from one another in any way. The woman has not been unfaithful, and the man isn't long suffering. Rashi is reading the Song of Songs through a lens so distorted as to render the actual poem irrelevant to the message Rashi insists that it carry.

As the ArtScroll editors make clear, Rashi's reading has become the standard allegory of the Song of Songs. This is true not only within Judaism but within Christianity as well. Given their faith in Jesus as the Son of God, Christian commentators tweak Rashi's allegory so that the Song of Songs is no longer an allegory of the love between God and Israel but an allegory of the love between Christ and his church.

> The surface or "literal" subject matter of the Song was the love that joins a bride and her betrothed, a sexual longing that the Song celebrates cheerfully. Understood in that way, however, the Song had little to say directly about the relation between God and "us"; and that relation of course defines the basic interest—the agenda—that Jews and Christians alike brought, and bring, to their reading of the Scriptures. Hence the traditional resort to allegory in interpretation of the Song: the love that it celebrates is treated as a figure of analogy for the love between God and the people of God, the Church. Thus in Christian allegory (or *anagogy*, "leading upward toward a higher meaning") the Bridegroom becomes Christ, the Word or Song of God, and the Bride becomes either the Church or, as Origen was the first to suggest, the individual believer. This suggestion of Origen—that the "spiritual" subject matter of the Song was not only the relation between Christ and the Church but also that between Christ and the individual soul—pretty well shaped the course of Christian interpretation of this book.[15]

Clearly these commentators found the Song of Songs too sexy for their tastes and did their best to smother the eroticism of the Song in a thick theological blanket. I do the opposite. For me, and for this reading of the Song of Songs, the eroticism is made explicit because it is essential to the message I believe the Song conveys. I am not adverse to allegory, but the allegory I explore here is not one of disembodied abstraction, but of a fully embodied awakening to Wisdom and the unity of God, woman, man, and nature that such an awakening entails.

Why the Bible Needs the Song of Songs

Given the incredible lengths to which traditional Bible commentators go to salvage the Song of Songs as a holy book, the question raised is why the Song of Songs was included in the Bible in the first place. If the erotic nature of the Song is so alien to the rest of the Bible, why make it part of the Bible at all? The Hebrew Bible makes reference to many books known to the compilers of the Bible that didn't make it into the Bible, so why not put the Song of Songs among the excluded books?[16]

According to noted Jewish historian Gerson Cohen, "From the point of view of the Jews of early rabbinic times [the time of the canon's compiling] without such a work as the Song of Songs the Bible was not quite complete."[17] The reason for this, Cohen says, was the Bible's already entrenched habit of commanding the Jews to love their God and of referring to the relationship between God and Israel as that between a husband and wife, a relationship unique among the peoples of the ancient Near East. While it was common for people of that time to address their gods in such terms as creator, king, lord, healer, or lawgiver, referring to God as spouse or lover was something only the Jews seemed to do.[18]

Deuteronomy 6:5 is perhaps the most famous admonition to love God, "You must love YHVH your God with all your heart and with all your soul and with all your strength."[19] Four chapters later, in Deuteronomy 10:12, we learn a bit more about what it means to love God: "And now, O Israel, what is it that YHVH your God demands of you? It is to revere YHVH your God, to walk only in God's paths, to love God, and to serve YHVH your God with all your heart and soul."

While the command to love God is clear, it appears that the Israelites often had a difficult time doing so. In Judges 2:17, we learn that the people "whored" (zanu, from zonah, "prostitute") after other Gods. In Hosea 2:9, Israel is likened to a married woman who takes on other lovers but who decides to return to her husband, God. A few verses later, in 2:21–22, God welcomes the reunion saying, "And I will betroth you to Me forever. Through righteousness and justice, in loyalty of love, I will betroth you to Me. I will betroth you to Me in faithfulness, and you will know YHVH."

Of all the prophets who use the imagery of bride and groom to speak of the relationship of Israel and her God, it may be Jeremiah who gives us the clearest hint as to why the Song of Songs was a necessary part of the Hebrew canon. In Jeremiah 2:2, God says, "I recall the devotion of your youth, your bridal love, how you followed Me through the wilderness in a land that was not sown."

What was that young love between God and Israel like? What is it that God remembers? The Song of Songs is the only book that can tell us that, and hence its inclusion in the Hebrew Bible is secured. As Gerson Cohen explains:

> In other words, whereas the other books of the Bible do indeed proclaim the bond of love between Israel and the Lord, only the Song of Songs is a dialogue of love, a conversation between a man and God that gives religious faith a kind of intensity no other form of expression can.[20]

That intensity of love begged for interpretation, and this led to a wide variety of allegorical readings. As Rashi's near contemporary Saadia Gaon (d. 942), the chief rabbi (gaon) of the Rabbinic Academy, put it in his own commentary to the Song of Songs:

> Know, my brother, that you will find great differences in interpretation of the Song of Songs. In truth they differ because the Song of Songs resembles locks to which the keys have been lost.[21]

Different allegories provide different keys, and while some fit better than others, there is no single key that all readers embrace. It is my opinion that reading the Song of Songs as an allegory of love between Wisdom and the seeker of Wisdom is one of the lost keys needed to unlock its message. In reading the Song this way, I am drawing on the work of two other commentators: the rabbinic sage Yehudah Abravanel (1465–1525), who read the Song of Songs as a dialogue between Lady Wisdom and King Solomon, and, some four hundred years later, the German biblical scholar Gottfried Kuhn, who adapted Abravanel's reading by exchanging Solomon for a generic seeker after Wisdom, the approach I am taking here.

Beyond Gender

For me, the Song of Songs is a celebration of the human relationship with Wisdom. The woman in the Song is *Chochmah*, Lady Wisdom. The man in the Song, Lady Wisdom's lover, is the seeker of Wisdom. But be careful. When I say that the seeker is the man in the Song, I do not mean to say that only men may be seekers. On the contrary, Wisdom calls out to all humanity (Proverbs 8:1) and invites everyone to her feast of instruction and insight (Proverbs 9:2–6).

Seekers are not defined by gender. This is why I shy away from masculine terminology in my translation and commentary and speak instead of "you." You, the reader, regardless of your gender identity or lack thereof, are the seeker.

Of course the Song of Songs employs the standard heterosexual trope common at the time of its composition, but that shouldn't limit our understanding of the Song for our time. Hebrew is a gendered language: things are either masculine or feminine, but this quality often has nothing to do with maleness or femaleness. For example the human body, *guf* in Hebrew, is masculine regardless of whether we are referring to a male body or a female body. Similarly, the vast majority of Hebrew words dealing with matters of the spirit, words like *nefesh* (soul) and *neshamah* (spirit), are feminine regardless of the gender of the person about whose soul or spirit we are speaking. For me, the Song of Songs is about the realization of Wisdom through the unification of the spiritual (feminine) and the physical (masculine), and not simply the male and the female.

Through My Flesh I See God

Unlike other allegorists, I am careful not to lose or allegorize away the eroticism of the Song. I do this because I believe there is an eroticism to the search for Wisdom and an ecstasy that is attained when Wisdom is embraced and lover and Beloved—the physical and the spiritual, the masculine and the feminine—become one.

Part of the genius of the Song of Songs is that it affirms the body as integral to the search for wisdom. As Job reminds us, "Through my flesh I see God" (19:26). The goal of the search isn't to escape your body and unite with Wisdom in some nonphysical realm, but to find Wisdom through the body and awaken to the holiness and wholeness of physical and spiritual together as a single reality. In this way the Song of Songs is a celebration of the union of the seeker of Wisdom with Lady Wisdom herself.

> This oneness heals all divisions and fuses all "separate" pow-
> ers and brings into the union of Sacred Marriage all the "male"
> and "female" powers of the self, unites and fuses intellect and
> divine love, imagination and ecstasy, the spirit and the body, the
> laws of the heart and the structures of mind, the light and every
> breath, gesture, thought, and emotion lived in its truth. What is
> born from this fusion, this Sacred Marriage of all the "separate"
> powers of heart, mind, body, and soul is the Sacred Androgyne,
> the one who in his or her being realizes the total interpenetra-
> tion ... of all normally "opposed" or "contradictory" qualities.
> This Sacred Androgyne—birthed in ... "bridal Chamber," the
> place of fusion between "male" and "female"—is a divinized
> human divine being free of all normal categories of "male" and
> "female" because it exists in a unity that contains, absorbs,
> "uses," and ecstatically transcends both.[22]

A Note on Translation and Presentation

The Song of Songs contains a variety of voices: Lady Wisdom, the seeker, Wisdom's companions whom she calls the daughters of Jerusalem, Wisdom's half-brothers, and the city guards. Distinguishing one from the other four can be challenging, and not all translators and commentators on the Song agree as to who is speaking when. To make the voices as clear as possible, each voice is noted at the top of page—both the translation page and its facing commentary page.

Translation from one language to another is as much art as science. It is not a matter of substituting English words for their Hebrew equivalents, but of trying to understand the sense of the text and finding just the right English word to make it clear. With the Song of Songs there is the added challenge of dealing with sexual innuendo and euphemism. The Song of Songs is a deeply erotic poem that employs lightly coded sexual imagery to speak to the union of Lady Wisdom and those who seek her. To merely crack the code and replace it with explicit sexual language would be to strip the Song of its poetry, beauty, genius, and mystery. In order to preserve these I have done my best to honor the metaphors used by the poet, employing the commentary page to unpack the imagery and explore the sexual mysticism at the heart of the Song.

As with all my books of translation and commentary, I urge those who can to refer to the original Hebrew text of the Song of Songs to see how I have used it. And I urge all readers to consult a variety of translations of the Song to see how else one might read this glorious poem.

☐ God's Daughter
Wisdom as the Divine Feminine

Given the centrality of *Chochmah*, Lady Wisdom, to this reading of Song of Songs, we would be wise to take a moment to understand just who she is. According to the book of Job, Wisdom is the means by which God created the universe: "God looked and took note of her" (Job 28:27). In other words, God looked to Wisdom to discover both the form and function of the universe. Wisdom, therefore, is the way nature is nature.

In Latin, the way nature is nature is called *natura naturans*, "nature naturing." What arises from nature naturing is called *natura naturata*, "created nature." The capacity of nature to birth humans, for example, is *natura naturans*, while any specific human is an expression of *natura naturata*.

Natura naturans is similar to the Chinese notion of Tao: "For Tao is itself the always—so, the fixed, the unconditioned, that which 'is of itself' and for no cause 'so.'"[1]

> The Tao that can be trodden is not the enduring and unchanging Tao. The name that can be named is not the enduring and unchanging name. (Conceived of as) having no name, it is the Originator of heaven and earth; (conceived of as) having a name, it is the Mother of all things.[2]

The Tao without a name is *natura naturans*, the creativity of the universe. The Tao with a name is *natura naturata*, creation itself.

A parallel understanding of this in Hinduism is the relationship of *Nirguna Brahman*, ultimate reality without form, and *Saguna Brahman*, ultimate reality with form. In Christianity, the same idea is expressed in the Prologue to the Gospel according to John:

17

In the beginning was Logos, and Logos was with God, and Logos was God. This one was in the beginning with God. All things came into being through Logos, and apart from Logos not one thing came into being that has come into being. In Logos was life, and the life was the light of humanity. (1:1–4)

Natura naturans informs *natura naturata*; *Nirguna Brahman* informs *Saguna Brahman*, the Unnamable Tao informs the nameable Tao, and God informs Logos. In the Hebrew Bible, the same dynamic exists between *YHVH* and *Chochmah*, the ultimate reality beyond name and form manifesting as the reality of name and form.

Most English translations of the Hebrew Bible render *YHVH* as "Lord." While this translation is terribly misleading, it has its origins in ancient Rabbinic tradition. The early Rabbis prohibited the pronunciation of *YHVH* and substituted the Hebrew *Adonai* instead. *Adonai* does mean "Lord," which explains the use of "Lord" in our English Bibles, but substituting *Adonai* for *YHVH* actually inverts the true meaning of *YHVH*.

Adonai is a masculine noun suggesting and enforcing the patriarchal hierarchy of power and privilege enjoyed by the Rabbis themselves. Rabbis were men, and exclusively so; therefore *YHVH* was male, and exclusively so. Rabbis were the pinnacle of power in Rabbinic society; therefore God was the pinnacle of power in creation. The Rabbis literally created a God in their own image who would, not surprisingly, support their own status and power. No wonder they read the Song of Songs as a celebration of themselves. But *YHVH* has nothing to do with any of this.

YHVH isn't a noun, but a verb: a form of the Hebrew verb "to be." As a verb, *YHVH* supports no hierarchy or power structure. Indeed, when Moses asks for the meaning of *YHVH* in Exodus 3:13–14, the Hebrew Bible defines *YHVH* as *Ehyeh asher Ehyeh*, not the static "I Am What I Am" of so many English translations of the Hebrew Bible, but the dynamic "I Am Becoming What I Am Becoming" of the Hebrew itself.

YHVH is an activity, be-*ing* itself rather than a being or even a supreme being. To borrow from Saint Paul in the book of Acts, "God is that in whom we live and move and have our being" (17:28). *YHVH* is *natura naturans*, *Nirguna Brahman*, the Tao without a name, God. From *YHVH* comes *natura naturata*, *Saguna Brahman*, the Tao with a name, Logos, and Wisdom. And because Wisdom comes from *YHVH*, Wisdom can lead us back to *YHVH* or, more accurately still, awaken us to our ever-present unity in, with, and as *YHVH*.

Who Is Lady Wisdom?

I am the deep grain of creation, the subtle current of life.
God fashioned me before all things:
I am the blueprint of creation.
I was there from the beginning,
from before there was a beginning.
I am independent of time and space, earth and sky.
I was there before depth was conceived,
before springs bubbled with water,
before the shaping of mountains and hills,
before God fashioned the earth and its bounty,
before the first dust settled on the land.
When God prepared the heavens, I was there.
When the circle of the earth was etched into the face of the deep,
I was there.
When the stars and planets soared into their orbit,
when the deepest oceans found their level
and the dry land established the shores, I was there.
I stood beside God as firstborn and friend.
My nature is joy, and I gave God constant delight.
Now that the world is inhabited, I rejoice in it.
I will be your true delight if you will heed my teachings.
Follow me and be happy.
Practice my discipline and grow wise

(PROVERBS 8:22–32)

It is with this passage that we are introduced to Lady Wisdom. While the gender of the speaker cannot be discerned in the English translation, the Hebrew is clear: the speaker is *Chochmah*, Lady Wisdom, and hence all the pronouns and verbs referring to Wisdom in the passage are feminine. The grammar of this and every passage that speaks of, to, about, or for Wisdom always uses the feminine form.

Wisdom is the firstborn of God, and from her comes the ten thousand things of creation. As Proverbs tells us, her way is the way of truth and justice (8:7–8), qualities hitherto associated with God. Her essence is itself pure delight, and she delights in humanity (8:30–31). One who finds her finds life (8:35). Compare this to Jesus when he says, "I am the way and the truth and the life. No one comes to the Father except through me" (Gospel according to John 14:6, NIV). Saint Paul makes the connection between Jesus and Wisdom quite plain: "Christ is the power of God and the wisdom of God" (1 Corinthians 1:24, NIV). What becomes the male Christ in the Christian Scriptures was originally the female *Chochmah* in the Hebrew Bible.

Wisdom is the way God manifests in and as creation. Uniting with Wisdom, as the Song of Songs invites us to do, is a way of uniting with life and the Source from which life arises. As Hebrew Bible scholar Gerhard von Rad explains:

It is correct to say that wisdom is the form in which Jahweh's will and his accompanying of man (i.e., his salvation) approaches man. Wisdom is the essence of what man needs for a proper life, and of what God grants him. Still, the most important thing is that wisdom does not turn towards man in the shape of an "It," teaching, guidance, salvation or the life, but of a person, a summoning "I." So wisdom is truly the form in which Jahweh makes himself present and in which he wishes to be sought by man. "Whoso finds me, finds life" (Prov. 8:35). Only Jahweh can speak in this way.[3]

I cannot emphasize enough the importance of this observation by von Rad that we are not talking about an abstract principle—wisdom with a lowercase "w"—but about a person—Wisdom with an uppercase "W." The personification of Lady Wisdom allows us to become intimate with her in ways we could not if she were merely a set of principles or ethical guidelines for right living.

We personify Wisdom because on a deep and subconscious level we know her to be the "Other" with whom we long to unite. She is not an abstraction but our Beloved. She is not to be thought about but physically embraced in a manner that reveals YHVH to us.

The Wisdom of Solomon, a Jewish text written in Greek sometime in the second or first century BCE, defines Wisdom this way:

> She is intelligent, holy, unique, subtle, flowing, transparent, and pure;
> she is distinct, invulnerable, good, keen, irresistible, and gracious;
> she is humane, faithful, sure, calm, all-powerful, all-seeing,
> and available to all who are intelligent, pure, and altogether simple.
> She is the mobility of movement;
> she is the transparent nothing that pervades all things.
> She is the breath of God,
> a clear emanation of Divine Glory.
> No impurity can stain her.
> She is God's spotless mirror reflecting eternal light,
> and the image of divine goodness.
> Although she is one,
> she does all things.
> Without leaving herself
> she renews all things.
> Generation after generation she slips into holy souls,
> making them friends of God, and prophets;
> for God loves none more than they who dwell with Wisdom.
> She is more beautiful than the sun,
> and the constellations pale beside her.
> Compared to light, she yet excels it.

For light yields to dark,
while she yields to nothing.
She stretches mightily throughout the cosmos
and guides the whole universe for its benefit.

(WISDOM OF SOLOMON 7:22–8:1)

Wisdom isn't limited to the spiritual sphere, nor is her concern with God's Chosen People alone. She is the mother of all life and is concerned with all life. Like Jesus, she sends her apostles (all women, in the case of Wisdom) to reach out to all humanity and invites us to join her in table fellowship:

Wisdom's house rests on many pillars.
It is magnificent and easy to find.
Inside, she has cooked a fine meal and sweetened her wine with water.
Her table is set.
She sends maidens to the tallest towers to summon you.
To the simple they call: *Come, enter here.*
To those who lack understanding they say:
Come, eat my food, drink my wine.
Abandon your empty life, and walk in the way of understanding.

(PROVERBS 9:1–6)

Wisdom's goal isn't to bring you to one set of beliefs or another but to make you wise. What does it mean to be wise? In the Wisdom of Solomon, the writer defines it this way:

Simply I learned from Wisdom: the design of the universe, the force of its elements, the nature of time—beginnings and endings, the shifting of the sun and the changing of seasons and cycles of years, the positions of stars, the nature of animals and the tempers of beasts, the power of the wind, and the thoughts of human beings, the medicinal uses of plants and roots. These and even deeper more hidden things I learned, for Wisdom, the Shaper of All, taught me.

(WISDOM OF SOLOMON 7:7–22)

But more prosaically, Wisdom teaches us physics, chemistry, astronomy, biology, ethnology, meteorology, psychology, pharmacology, and more. Wisdom reveals to us the explicit and the implicit, the visible and the hidden. How can she do this? Because she is the means by which the universe came to be.

Wisdom and *Shekhinah*

Just as the Logos is both with God and God in John's Prologue, over time *Chochmah* shifts from being a separate entity who exists with God to being an expression of God: God as we experience God here on earth. The presence of God is called *Shekhinah*, and she, no less than *Chochmah*, is feminine. It may be their shared gender that led the two to be understood as one.

In Proverbs 8:22, Wisdom tells us she is God's daughter, the first of God's creations, established before the universe. Eight verses later she tells us she is the architect of creation, but in neither case is she synonymous with the Creator. The intimacy between God and Wisdom intensifies but still remains dualistic in the second-century text the Wisdom of Solomon, where the relationship between God and Wisdom changes from daughter to lover. Solomon says of Wisdom:

> She embraces the universe in its infinite power
> and orders all things for their benefit.
> Wisdom I loved and sought after her from my youth,
> to take her as my bride.
> I was intoxicated by her beauty.
> She proclaimed her noble birth
> and that she lived with God,
> and *YHVH* loved her.
>
> (WISDOM OF SOLOMON 8:1–3)

Philo (20 BCE–50 CE), the first-century Jewish philosopher and Hebrew Bible commentator, makes the connection with God even more intimate:

And thus the Demiurge [God as Creator] who created our entire universe is rightly called the Father of all Created Things, while we call *Episteme/Sophia/*Wisdom mother, whom God knew and through this knowing created all reality, albeit not in human fashion. However, she received the divine seed and bore with labor the one and beloved son ... the ripe fruit of this world.[4]

We can see in Philo the beginnings of John's theology and even a prototype of the later Christian teaching of virgin birth, with Mary taking the place of *Sophia/*Wisdom. While Philo is willing to follow the Hebrew Bible's teaching that Wisdom is with God, he is not ready to take the leap that John does to affirm that Wisdom is God. This changes when talking of *Shekhinah.*

While Wisdom is related to God as either God's daughter or God's wife, *Shekhinah* is of God herself. The term is unique to Rabbinic literature starting in the first century BCE. The *Shekhinah* is God's dwelling—not the place in which God dwells, but any place that God dwells. Whenever you find yourself in the presence of God, you are in *Shekhinah*. Hence the Rabbis taught:

Rabbi Chalafta ben Dosa of Kfar Chanania teaches,
If ten people sit together and study Torah,
the *Shekhinah* rests among them....
This is also true of five.... It is also true of three....
It is also true of two.... This is even true of one, for it says,
"In every place where I cause My Name to be mentioned,
I will come to you and bless you."[5]

The *Shekhinah* is never separate from God, as Wisdom sometimes seems to be. Indeed, while the gender of *Shekhinah* is feminine, she is not personified as a woman in the early Rabbinic literature, though as we shall see, this changes over time.

The earliest example of Shekhinah as separate from God can be found in a Rabbinic commentary to Proverbs 22:29, "A hard worker can stand tall before kings; there is no greater honor than honest labor":

When the Sanhedrin gathered to strip King Solomon along with three other kings and four others of their place in the world to come, the *Shekhinah* stepped before the Holy One, blessed be God, and said to God, "Master of all worlds! Don't you see this hard worker standing before kings [meaning Solomon]? The Court would count him among the damned?" At that moment a heavenly voice spoke aloud, "He [Solomon] shall stand before kings and not as one of the damned."[6]

What is important to note here is that *Shekhinah*, like *Chochmah*, is separate from God in this passage and addresses God as a being in her own right. Given that both *Shekhinah* and *Chochmah* are referred to in the feminine, it isn't surprising that they eventually come to be seen as one in the same.

It is in Kabbalah, the teachings of Jewish mysticism, that we see what I take to be the deepest meaning of and connection between *Shekhinah*, Wisdom, and the Song of Songs.

The essence of the Kabbalistic idea of God ... lies in its resolutely dynamic conception of the Godhead: God's creative power and vitality develop in an unending movement of His nature, which flows not only outward into Creation but also back into itself.[7]

God is *YHVH*, the be-ing of all being. God is intrinsically creative, indeed is creativity itself. Yet, God is more than observable reality. God is also the source of that reality. The metaphor I find most helpful is that of the relationship between an ocean, the waving of the ocean, and the waves that arise from that waving. Speaking metaphorically and not scientifically, God as Source is the ocean, God as Wisdom is the waving of the ocean, and God as *Shekhinah* is the wave that arises from that waving.

The Kabbalists resorted to the expedient of differentiating between two strata of the Godhead: one, its hidden being-in-itself, its immanence in the depths of its own being; and another, that of its

creative and active nature, thrusting outward toward expression....
The former stratum is designated in the language of the Kabbalists as *Ein-Sof*, the undifferentiated unity, the self-contained Root
of Roots in which all contradictions merge and dissolve. The latter substratum is the structure of the ten *Sefiroth*, which are the
sacred names—i.e., the various aspects of God—or the ten words
of Creation (*logoi*) by which everything was created.[8]

In the kabbalistic model of the *sefirot, Shekhinah* is the final manifestation and culmination of the divine activity: God as "simultaneously
mother, bride, and daughter."[9] In what is perhaps the earliest book of
Jewish mystical teaching, the third- or fourth-century *Book of Creation*
(*Sefer Yetzirah*), we find the following tale told by historian and philosopher Gershom Scholem:

> This is like a king who was in the innermost chamber of his apart-
> ments, and the number of rooms was thirty-two, and there was
> a path to every room. Did it behoove the king to allow everyone
> to enter his rooms by these paths? No! But did it behoove him
> not to show his pearls and jeweled settings and hidden treasures
> and beautiful things to all? No! What did the king do? He took
> his daughter and concentrated all paths in her and in her gar-
> ments [i.e., her manifestation], and he who wishes to enter the
> interior must look at her. And she is married to a king, and she
> was given to him as a gift. At times, in his great love for her, he
> calls her "my sister," for they come from one place; sometimes
> he calls her "my daughter," for she is his daughter; and some-
> times he calls her "my mother."[10]

Wisdom as *Shekhinah*

As Jewish thought works toward the unification of Wisdom and *Shekhinah*, it does so by reimagining *Shekhinah* as the feminine attribute of
God rather than the presence of God.

The final *Sefirah* descends to the earthly realm in the guise of *Shekhinah* mentioned in the Talmud and the "Wisdom" of the Bible. She is no longer God's presence, but is now a specific factor in His self-manifestation.[11]

Beyond Scholem's observation of the unity of *Shekhinah* and Wisdom, Rabbi Moshe ben Nachman (1194–1270), better known as Nachmanides or the Ramban, identifies *Shekhinah* with the "bride of the Song of Songs" and sees her as that in which "everything is in-gathered."[12]

The kabbalists referred to the manifestation of the *Shekhinah* in the world as "in everything" (*ba-kol*). She is "the light that emanates from the primal light which is *Chochmah*."[13] She is the same below as she is above; that is, she permeates the manifest world and the unmanifest Source from which and in which the manifest arises. In this, Scholem tells us, she resembles the Hindu goddess Shakti, the active energy of Shiva (God) manifesting as the externalized creation.[14]

Chochmah in her purest form is, in the minds of some kabbalists, *Koach Mah*, the potentiality of all creation—as yet unmanifest creativity, *natura naturans*. When Wisdom shifts from *natura naturans* to *natura naturata*, the unmanifest to the manifest, God without form to God with form, we speak of her as *Shekhinah*. In this sense the Divine Feminine permeates all reality, material and spiritual, physical and mental. She is imminent in, with, and as the world, binding all things together in her infinite being.[15]

☐ Back to the Garden
From Eve to the *Shulamite*

The medieval kabbalist Joseph Gikatilla (1248–ca. 1305) identified several women in the Hebrew Bible with the *Shekhinah*: "The *Shekhinah* in Abraham's time was called Sarah, in Isaac's time Rebecca, and in Jacob's time Rachel."[1] I would add two more to Gikatilla's list: in Adam's time she is called *Chavah* (Eve), and in Solomon's time (by which I mean the time portrayed in the Song of Songs) she is called the *Shulamite*, the Woman of Wholeness and Peace featured in the Song itself (Song of Songs 7:1).

Making this claim is part of the allegorical reading central to this book. So central, in fact, that one can read the Song of Songs as completing the Garden of Eden story told in the third chapter of Genesis. That story ends with humanity exiled from the Garden; the Song of Songs tells us how to return. To understand how this works, we have to retell the story of Eve in the context of Wisdom. Because the Garden of Eden story has traditionally been read in such a way as to place the burden of evil coming into the world on Eve and through Eve on all womankind, my reading of the story may appear a bit shocking. It is, however, more true to the actual Hebrew text than the conventional reading.

Chavah—Eve

Let's begin with the creation of woman in Genesis 2. God sees that "it is not good that *adam* ["earthling," from *adamah*, "earth"] is alone; I will make for *adam* an *eizer k'nego*, a helper of equal worth" (Genesis 2:18).

This phrase "a helper of equal worth" is a bit awkward in English, but not so in Hebrew. *Eizer* means "helper." *K'negdo* means something like

29

the loyal opposition. The role of the woman is to stand in loving opposition to the man and in this way overcome the aloneness God seeks to avoid. It is this aloneness, this sense of separation, that will prove pivotal in the exile of the man (but not the woman) from the Garden.[2]

Prior to the creation of woman, God fashions all the animals of the earth and brings each to *adam* to see if any of them can overcome *adam*'s aloneness. Sexual union was the means by which aloneness was to be overcome, but according to the Rabbis, no animal completed the human.[3] Only after the failure of the animals to overcome *adam*'s aloneness does God put *adam* to sleep, and from *adam*'s side (the Hebrew is *tzeila*, "side," not "rib") God draws out woman (*ishah*) (Genesis 2:21–22). When *adam* awakes (from having slept with this new creation?) things prove different: "This time it is bone of my bones and flesh of my flesh. This shall be called *ishah* [woman] for from *ish* [man] was she taken" (Genesis 2:23).

Despite the claim that *ishah* came from *ish*, that woman came from man, the Hebrew text actually reveals that both *ish* and *ishah* came from *adam*, the singular human. The words *ish* and *ishah* are used here for the first time; neither comes before the other. Man and woman both come from *adam* and are aspects of *adam*, and only when they unite with one another can they achieve the unity from which they originally derived.

Unity Lost

In Genesis 1:27 we learn that *adam*, though grammatically masculine and singular, is both masculine and feminine. While the simple reading of this text, reinforced in Genesis 5:2, is that God created two sexes from the very beginning, this reading becomes problematic in light of Genesis 2:7, when God forms a single earthling (*adam*) from the dust of the earth.

To harmonize the two stories, the ancient Rabbis imagined *adam* as androgynous or as conjoined twins:

"You have formed me front and back" (Psalm 139:5). Rabbi Jeremiah ben Eleazar said, "When the Holy One, blessed be He, created the first *adam*, He created it with both male and female sex organs, as it is written, *Male and female He created them, and He called their name adam* (Genesis 5:2)." Rabbi Samuel ben Nahmani then said, "When the Holy One, blessed be He, created the first *adam*, He created him with two faces, then slit him and made him two backs—a back for each side."[4]

The unity of *adam* was lost with the splitting of *adam* (earthling) into *ish* (man) and *ishah* (woman). The result of that lost unity is portrayed in the Garden of Eden story.

The Relationship of *Ish* and *Ishah*

To understand the relationship between *ish* and *ishah*, we must unpack the meaning of the two words. As taught to me decades ago, the word *ish* (*aleph-yud-shin*), "man," is derived from *eish* (*aleph-shin*), "fire." What differentiates "man" from "fire," *ish* from *eish*, is the letter *yud*, which is the first letter of the divine name YHVH (*Yud-Hei-Vav-Hei*) and which stands for *yada*, "unitive knowing." As long as a man is informed by the unity of God, woman, man, and nature, he is an *ish*, a holy fire if you like, bringing light and warmth wherever he goes. Awakening the *yud* is part of a man's spiritual practice, and since *yada* is also a euphemism for sexual intercourse, one way of achieving unity consciousness is through sexual union. As we shall see, the Song of Song speaks directly to this practice.

In Hebrew, *ishah* (woman) is also composed of three letters: *aleph-shin-hei*. *Ishah* lacks the letter *yud* and instead ends with the letter *hei* Does the absence of the *yud* in *ishah* mean that woman lacks this intimate knowing? In a way it does: woman doesn't *have* wisdom; woman *is* wisdom.

The vowel sound *ee*, made by the presence of the letter *yud* between the *aleph* and the *shin* in *ish* (man) is not absent in *ishah* but internalized and integrated to the point of not needing to be marked by a separate letter at all. This point will have great importance as our story progresses.

Because *ishah* has internalized the *yud* of *YHVH* and *yada* (knowing), *ishah* contains the letter *hei*, the second and fourth letters in the divine name *YHVH*, and the second letter of the divine name *Yah*, *yud-hei* (as in *hallelu-Yah*, "praise Yah, praise God"). When *ish* (with the *yud*) is united with *ishah* (with the *hei*), the fully realized divine, *Yah*, manifests. The union of the woman and her lover in the Song of Songs is the union of *hei* and *yud*. The union of Wisdom (the feminine principle) and the seeker of Wisdom (the masculine principle) in our spiritual practice is the same. In both cases we have the possibility of realizing God through ecstasy.

Furthermore, when the letter *hei* appears at the end of a word as it does in *ishah*, it often denotes direction. While *ish* (man) is a holy fire, he lacks direction. *Ishah*, on the other hand, includes both the holy fire of *yud* and the directional activity of *hei*. So *ishah* implies not only that the woman has internalized unitive knowing and the wisdom that comes with it, but also that she uses that knowing to offer direction to *ish*, who lacks it. It is in doing so that she becomes *eizer k'negdo*, the helper of equal worth.

Both man and woman have the potential for unitive knowing, but only the woman knows how to use it, which may explain why it is that the man leaves "his father and his mother and clings to his woman in the way of becoming one flesh" (Genesis 2:24) and why it is that the woman in both the Garden of Eden and the Song of Songs directs the man to Wisdom.

To fully understand what the Bible is saying, we have to make a shift from "male" and "female" to "masculine" and "feminine"—from physical sexes to psycho-spiritual archetypes. *Adam*, the original human of Genesis 1:27, is both masculine and feminine. The parable of the Garden of Eden speaks to the separation these two forces. The parable of the Song of Songs speaks to their reunification. Both texts use the image of a woman and a man to tell their story, and both should be read more deeply if their spiritual meaning is to be revealed. With this in mind, let's go more deeply into the Genesis story.

The Naked Truth

Chapter 2 of Genesis closes with the observation that both the man and the woman were naked (*arumim*), and neither was ashamed (2:25). Chapter 3 opens with a description of the serpent as the most *arum* of any creature God had made (3:1). While it is common for English translations to render the Hebrew *arum* as "naked" when referring to the humans (*arumim* is the plural of *arum*) and as "cunning" or "devious" when referring to the snake in the very next verse, doing so is arbitrary and blinds us to the true meaning of the story.

The humans and the serpent, alone among all creatures, are naked. What can this mean? How is a serpent naked in a way that corresponds to how humans are naked? I suggest we read "naked" in the sense of "innocent." The serpent was innocent and not devious. In fact, playing with *gematria*, Hebrew numerology, a common tool of Rabbinic interpretation of the Hebrew Bible, we discover that the Hebrew word for "serpent" (*nachash* in Hebrew: *nun* [50] + *chet* [8] + *shin* [300] = 358) has the same numerological value as that for "messiah" (*mashiach*: *mem* [40] + *shin* [300] + *yud* [10] + *chet* [8] – 358). The rules of *gematria* allow the reader to substitute words sharing the same numerical value: the snake is the messiah disguised as a serpent!

But the messiah wouldn't seek to trick the humans into sinning, so some other goal must lie behind the serpent's efforts to get the woman to eat of the Tree of Knowledge of Good and Evil. The goal, I suggest, is to open the eyes of the man and the woman and to move them beyond their childlike state into adulthood. To achieve this goal, the messiah takes on the shape of a serpent, the most innocent and thus trustworthy creature in the Garden, and seeks out the woman to carry out his plan.

Again we have to wonder why, in what is usually considered a patriarchal myth, does the serpent seek out *ishah* rather than *ish*, the woman rather than the man? Traditionally the answer has been that the woman's will is weaker than that of the man, and it is this reading that has become foundational to so much misogyny over the past thousands of years. But this isn't the only reading of the text.

The messiah/serpent sought out the woman rather than the man because the woman—*ishah*—is the one with the potential to realize the internalized *yud*, the unitive knowing that is at the heart of Wisdom, and then take action (the externalized *hei*) to move humanity in the direction of Wisdom. The serpent seeks out not the person most vulnerable to sin, but rather the person most capable of realizing Wisdom—the woman.

To Eat or Not to Eat, That Is the Question

The serpent urges the woman to eat from the Tree of Knowledge and to become like God, but she refuses (Genesis 3:5). She will not be cajoled into doing what she believes is forbidden. Then the Hebrew Bible tells us, "The woman perceived that the tree was good for eating and that it was a delight to the eyes, and that the tree was desirable as a means to Wisdom, and she took of its fruit and ate" (Genesis 3:6).

We tend to read this dawning realization as a single happening: the woman sees that the fruit of the Tree of Knowledge appears delicious, beautiful, and eye-opening. But this is not the only way to read the verse. Think of these as three clauses representing three distinct encounters with the Tree of Knowledge. First, the woman is attracted by the lusciousness of the fruit and the desire to consume it, but that isn't enough to make her do so. She masters her hunger and moves on without eating the fruit.

Sometime later she passes by the Tree again and this time perceives that the fruit is beautiful, and she desires to possess it. But beauty also fails to move her, so she again masters her passion and moves on without plucking the fruit. Only on a third encounter with the Tree does she sees that the Tree will make her wise, and only then does she consciously and deliberately eat of the Tree of Knowledge. It isn't that she has rationalized away the commandment to not eat of the Tree, but that she is willing to risk her very existence for the sake of Wisdom. In other words, her innate capacity for internalizing Wisdom is realized in her act of eating the fruit of the Tree of Knowledge.

Now think in terms of the woman in the Song of Songs. Just as the woman in the Garden broke the sole rule for living there, the woman in the Song breaks the customs of her day and makes love to her lover outside the boundaries of marriage. Just as the woman in the Garden eats the fruit of the Tree, the woman in the Song eats the fruit of her lover (Song of Songs 2:3). And just as the woman of the Garden offers the fruit of Wisdom to her man, so the woman of the Song offers the fruit of her body to her man. The difference between these women isn't their desire to feed their men, but the ability of their respective partners to properly accept what is offered.

While the woman in Genesis eats only after mastering her passions, her man acts very differently: "And she gave also to her man who was with her and he ate" (Genesis 3:6). The man eats without thinking. He blindly consumes; he acts from *eish*—fire, passion, and compulsivity— rather than from the *yud* of *ish*, the *yud* of *yada*, unitive knowing.

The mistake the woman makes is to assume that the man, who, after all, was right there with her, had reached the same level of consciousness that she had. She offers him Wisdom before he has mastered his baser instincts to consume and possess. Unlike in the Song of Songs where Wisdom and her lover are equally *eizer k'negdo* each to the other, work- ing with each other to bring each other to the fully embodied ecstasy of awakening, the *ish* in Genesis is incapable of fully realizing the gift offered him by the *ishah*. This is why there is no fear, punishment, or exile in the Song of Songs as there is in the Genesis story.

At the moment the woman and her man eat of the fruit of the Tree of Knowledge, their eyes are opened and they realize they are naked (Genesis 3:7). Notice that their nakedness evokes nothing but a desire to cover themselves. No shame is mentioned. But all that changes when God confronts the man in the Garden.

Hearing God approach, the two of them hide. God then calls to the man alone. Why? Because only the man poses a problem for God. The woman has fulfilled her nature as the embodiment of Wisdom; she has internalized the *yud* of unitive knowing and manifested the *hei* of holy action: she partook of the fruit of awakening to Wisdom, and she offered it (albeit prematurely) to her man. She is ready to lead. The man, on the other hand, is in a very different state. Put bluntly by the fifth-century church father Saint Augustine, where the woman is guided by Wisdom, the man is now ruled by his penis:

> These members [the penis] being moved and restrained not at our will, but by a certain independent autocracy, so to speak, are called "shameful." Their condition was different before sin ... because not yet did lust move those members without the will's consent.... But when [Adam] was stripped of grace ... there began to be in the movement of their bodily members a shame- less novelty which made nakedness indecent.[5]

Saint Augustine imagined that before eating from the Tree of Knowl- edge, the man could have impregnated the woman "without the seduc- tive stimulus of passion, with calmness of mind, and with no corruption of the innocence of the body.... It would have been possible to inject the semen into the womb through the female genitalia as innocently as the menstrual flow is now ejected."[6] And while tradition has blamed all of this on the woman, it is important to note that the Hebrew Bible does not.

God calls to the man, who blames his hiding on the fact of his naked- ness (Genesis 3:10). The man doesn't confess to eating the fruit, only to feeling fear over being naked. When challenged, the man blames the woman for his situation, and the woman blames the serpent. God punishes all three: the serpent must crawl on its belly, the woman must endure the pain of childbirth, and the man must toil mightily to bring forth the bounty of the earth (Genesis 3:14–19).

Immediately after this, Genesis 3:20 says, "The man called his woman *Chavah* [Eve], because she had become the mother of all the living" (*Chavah* means "living one" in Hebrew). This is an odd verse, and there is no reason for it. It doesn't move the story forward or even make sense. What it does is link *Chavah* to *Chochmah*, Eve to Wisdom, for the way *Chavah*, the helpmate, is the mother of all the living isn't that she births them into life but that she births them into Wisdom—the wisdom her man could not internalize.

The story resumes, and God worries aloud, "Now that the man has become *k'achad mimennu*, knowing good and evil, he might reach out and take also of the Tree of Life, and eat and live forever!" (Genesis 3:22). In standard English translations of the Bible, the Hebrew phrase *k'achad mimennu* is rendered "like one of us"—in other words, "like a god." But if this were the case, the Hebrew would be *k'echad mimennu*. *Achad* means "unique," and a better reading of the Hebrew would be this: "The man—and not the woman—has become unique, no longer one with us, but separate from us, alienated from us, and hence fearful of us, and a danger to himself. If the man were now to eat of the Tree of Life and attain immortality, he would be locked into this state of psycho-spiritual exile forever."

The fact that God is concerned only with the man and not with the woman suggests that God recognizes that she has internalized Wisdom and reached her potential as *ishah*, while the man is dangerously close to being permanently condemned to *eish*, a consuming fire. It is for this reason that God exiles the man, but again not the woman. The Hebrew and the English are equally clear: "So God banished him from the Garden of Eden" (Genesis 3:23). Him and not her. Eve is not exiled at all.

Following the man's exile from the Garden, God places fierce cherubim with an ever-turning sword of fire "to guard" (*lishmor*) the way to the Tree of Life (Genesis 3:24). While it is customary to understand the cherubim as defenders of the Tree, empowered to keep the man from returning to it, the text itself is far less clear on this matter. The Hebrew *lishmor* simply means "to protect." One could read the Hebrew Bible as saying that the role of the cherubim with the flaming sword is to protect the way back to the Tree so that when the man is ready to return the way will be lighted and cleared for him. When will the man be ready to return? When he has achieved what the woman has achieved: the internalization of Wisdom.

Remember, according to Proverbs 8:22 Wisdom isn't a late addition to creation, but the way creation is created. Wisdom is intrinsic to all reality. What Lady Wisdom of Proverbs, the mother of all the living of Genesis, and the Woman of Wholeness and Peace of the Song of Songs offer is the awakening of this innate Wisdom.

The Shulamite

While the *ishah* in Genesis is called *Chavah*, mother of all the living, this is more a title than a name. Similarly with the woman in the Song of Songs. She, too, has a title but not a name: the *Shulamite* (Song of Songs 7:1). It is the woman's lover who calls her this, just as it is Adam who names Eve, so these titles may reflect the perspective of the seeker rather than the woman herself. The meaning of *Chavah* as "mother of all the living" is explained in the story itself, but the meaning of *Shulamite* is left for us to uncover.

In Hebrew the root letters of *Shulamite—sh-l-m—*are the same root letters as the name *Shlomo*, Solomon. Some commentators take this as a poetic way of linking the woman to the man in the Song, who they take to be King Solomon. Reading the male lover as Solomon, however, is a stretch. While Solomon is mentioned in the Song (1:1, 8:11–12), he is never directly linked to the male lover. Yet, I think the root letters of *Shulamite* do tell us who she is.

The letters *sh-l-m* are also the root letters of the Hebrew words *shaleim* and *shalom*, "wholeness" and "peace." If, as I am positing in this book, the female Beloved in the Song of Songs is *Chochmah*, Lady Wisdom, and Lady Wisdom, like *Chavah*, is the mother of all things—the way nature natures—then we might understand the *Shulamite* as the Woman of *Shaleim* and *Shalom*, the Woman of Wholeness and Peace.

The same title could be given to *Chochmah* in the book of Proverbs, for it is through her that the whole of creation happens, and "all her paths are peace" (3:17).

Lady Wisdom calls us to share a feast with her in the book of Proverbs (9:2–5). Lady Wisdom as the *Shulamite* is the feast in the Song of Songs. The *Shulamite* is called a garden in the Song of Songs (4:12), and hence union with her is returning to the Garden from which Adam was exiled. This is to say that the Song of Songs completes the story of Eden by showing us the way back to the Garden.

Union with Wisdom is presented to us in the Song of Songs as sexual union because it is through sexual intimacy (*yada*) that one achieves unitive knowing (again, *yada*).

The full splendor of sexual experience does not reveal itself with a new mode of attention to the world in general. On the other hand, the sexual relationship is a setting in which the full opening of attention may rather easily be realized because it is so immediately rewarding. It is the most common and dramatic instance of union between oneself and the other. But to serve as a means of initiation to the "one body" of the universe, it requires what we have called a contemplative approach. This is not love "without desire" in the sense of love without delight, but love which is not contrived or willfully provoked as an escape from the habitual empty feeling of the isolated ego.[7]

In other words, love must be spontaneous and unrestrained, and sex must be no less so. This is the love the *Shulamite*, Lady Wisdom, the archetype of the Divine Feminine, shares with her lover in the Song of Songs.

☐ Through My Flesh I See God
The Song of Songs as Jewish Maithuna

Maithuna is a Sanskrit word meaning "sexual union" and is often spoken of in the context of yoga. *Yoga* is the Sanskrit word for "union," more specifically the union of the self with the All, or Atman with Brahman. *Maithuna* is one way to celebrate this union. In the case of the Song of Songs, "eroticism becomes worship in the context of grace."[1]

The union of self and other and of self and All is a given. You are at this very moment part of the infinite singularity that is reality. You may call this Brahman, God, Spirit, Tao, Mother, or any number of other names, but the simple fact is, as the Chandogya Upanishad, one of the great texts of Hindu philosophy, put it over twenty-six hundred years ago, *Tat tvam Assi*: You are That.

If you are a poet, you will see clearly that there is a cloud floating in this sheet of paper. Without a cloud, there will be no rain; without rain, the trees cannot grow; and without trees, we cannot make paper. The cloud is essential for the paper to exist. If the cloud is not here, the sheet of paper cannot be here either. So we can say that the cloud and the paper *inter-are*. "Interbeing" is a word that is not in the dictionary yet, but if we combine the prefix "inter-" with the verb "to be," we have a new verb, *inter-be*....

If we look into this sheet of paper even more deeply, we can see the sunshine in it. If the sunshine is not there, the forest cannot grow. In fact, nothing can grow. Even we cannot grow without sunshine. And so, we know that the sunshine is also in this sheet of paper. The paper and the sunshine inter-are. And if we continue to look, we can see the logger who cut the tree and brought it to the mill to be transformed into paper.... And the logger's father and mother are in it too....

Looking even more deeply, we can see we are in it too.... "To be" is to inter-be. You cannot just be by yourself alone. You have to inter-be with every other thing. This sheet of paper is, because everything else is.[2]

Maithuna is not a way to achieve interbeing, it is a way to celebrate inter-being. The Song of Songs is not a method whereby one achieves union with Wisdom incarnate as the *Shulamite*, the Woman of Wholeness and Peace, it is a way of awakening to that union. What the *Shulamite* offers the seeker in her garden is what *ishah* (woman) offered *ish* (man) in the Garden of Eden: the opportunity to awaken to the union of opposites. Where the man was not ready to fully embrace this gift in the Garden of Eden, the seeker is led through a careful cultivation of ecstasy that allows for the awakening of Wisdom in the Garden that is the *Shulamite*.

In the practice of *maithuna*, the female partner takes on the role of Shakti, the active, immanent, creativity of the Divine, and the male partner takes on the role of Shiva, the transcendent aspect of the Divine. The union of the two is a slow process of awakening through the body. In the Song of Songs this entire process is directed by the woman, by Wisdom, breaking the taboos of the times.

> The woman plays a sexually aggressive role; she violates boundaries by searching in the streets for her beloved; she also uses a bold, incestuous metaphor as she addresses her love: "If only it could be as with a brother, as if you had nursed at my mother's breast; then I could kiss you when I met you in the street, and no one would despise me" (8:1). But the watchmen who find her in the street beat her, as if to control her unconventional behavior (5:7), much as her brothers force her to guard their vineyards (1:6).[3]

In the context of the Song, the command of the *Shulamite* to the daughters of Jerusalem not to wake or disturb the lovers until they have reached the consummation of their union (2:7, 3:5, 8:4) could be read as a warning to neophytes not to mistake the *maithuna* of the Song for simple human coupling, as Adam mistook eating the fruit offered him by *ishah* for the simple act of consuming. *Maithuna* is a spiritual practice that employs the body but still requires concentration of mind.

In the context of Jewish mysticism, *maithuna* may be likened to reunion (*tikkun*), awakening to the non-dual nature of reality.

> When they [*ish* and *ishah*] are joined they appear as one actual body. From here we learn that a man alone appears as half a body ... and similarly the woman. When they are joined as one, everything appears as one actual body, Thus, when the male joins with the female, everything is one body, and all the worlds are in joy for they are all blessed from the complete body.[4]

The image presented by this practice mirrors that of *yab-yum* (Tibetan for "father-mother"), with the male deity sitting with his female consort on his lap. The male in this setting symbolizes *karuna* (compassion) while the woman embodies *prajña* (wisdom).[5] In Hindu iconography the couple embracing is Shiva and Shakti.

According to Hindu scholar Ananda Coomaraswamy, the significance of the union of Shiva and Shakti is threefold. First, it represents "Rhythmic Play as the Source of all Movement within the Cosmos"; second, it releases humanity from the illusion of separation at the heart of our suffering; and third, it reminds us that this union, while taking place at the center of the universe, is taking place in your own heart as well.[6]

Lest you imagine I am imposing Indian sexual union imagery on Judaism, the Talmud tells us that once a year during the festival of Sukkot, the priests of the Temple would open the curtain that covered the Holy of Holies and reveal to the people two cherubim, one male and the other female, in sexual union. The priests would then cry out, "Look! You are beloved by God as the love between a man and woman!"[7]

Let me go one step further, however, and suggest that the Song of Songs, like the image of *yab-yum*, can be a map for a spiritual practice of sexual union as well. As the Baal Shem Tov, the founder of Hasidic Judaism, taught, "Prayer is a form of intercourse with *Shekhinah*."[8] The opposite, too, can be true: sex is a form of prayer. Rabbi Baruch of Kosov taught:

> I once heard a modest man bemoan the fact that it is human nature to have physical pleasure from sex. He preferred that there be no feeling of pleasure at all, so that he could have sex solely to fulfill the command of his creator.... Later, however, God favored me with a gift of grace, granting me understanding of the true meaning of sanctification during sexual intercourse: that it comes precisely from feeling physical pleasure. This secret is wondrous, deep, and awesome.[9]

Which leads me to this question: is the Song of Songs for straight women and men only?

Toward a Holy Androgyny

When speaking of the creation of *adam*, the first earthling, in Genesis 1:27, the Hebrew Bible says God created *adam* "male and female." The logical way to read this is to say God created man and woman at the same time. The problem with this reading is that just prior to telling us that God created "them," the Hebrew Bible says God created "him."

While many English translations avoid the confusion by changing "him" to "them," the Hebrew leaves us without any such wiggle room. How can God create *adam* singular (he) and then plural (them)? Problems such as these are ripe for interpretation. Indeed, Judaism thrives on such textual difficulties, using them to expand the meaning of the Hebrew Bible far beyond the plain reading of the text and into the furthest reaches of Rabbinic imagination. To take but one example apropos to our discussion, Rabbi Jeremiah son of Rabbi Eleazar claims that God

WIN A $100 GIFT CERTIFICATE!

Fill in this card and mail it to us—or fill it in online at

skylightpaths.com/feedback.html

—to be eligible for a $100 gift certificate for SkyLight Paths books.

SKYLIGHT PATHS PUBLISHING
SUNSET FARM OFFICES RTE 4
PO BOX 237
WOODSTOCK VT   05091-0237

Fill in this card and return it to us to be eligible for our quarterly drawing for a $100 gift certificate for SkyLight Paths books.

We hope that you will enjoy this book and find it useful in enriching your life.

Book title: _____

Your comments: _____

How you learned of this book: _____

If purchased: Bookseller _____

City _____ State _____

Please send me a free SkyLight Paths Publishing catalog. I am interested in: (check all that apply)

1. ☐ Spirituality
2. ☐ Mysticism/Kabbalah
3. ☐ Philosophy/Theology

4. ☐ Spiritual Texts
5. ☐ Religious Traditions (Which ones?) _____
6. ☐ Children's Books

7. ☐ Prayer/Worship
8. ☐ Meditation
9. ☐ Interfaith Resources

Name (PRINT) _____

Street _____

City _____ State _____ Zip _____

E-MAIL (FOR SPECIAL OFFERS ONLY) _____

Please send a SkyLight Paths Publishing catalog to my friend:

Name (PRINT) _____

Street _____

City _____ State _____ Zip _____

SKYLIGHT PATHS® Publishing Tel: (802) 457-4000 • Fax: (802) 457-4004

Available at better booksellers. Visit us online at www.skylightpaths.com

created the original earthling androgynous. Rabbi Samuel son of Rabbi Nahman disagreed, saying that *adam* was not androgynous but "double-faced," and joined along the back, what we today would call conjoined twins.[10]

My own reading of Genesis posits the original earthling as bisexual—physically, psychologically, and spiritually. *Adam* is the sacred androgyne, to use religious scholar Andrew Harvey's term, who actualizes the inter-being of feminine and masculine and who longs to be born in your body.

> This oneness heals all divisions and fuses all "separate" powers and brings into the union of Sacred Marriage all the "male" and "female" powers of the self, unites and fuses intellect and divine love, imagination and ecstasy, the spirit and the body, the laws of the heart and the structures of mind, the light and every breath, gesture, thought, and emotion lived in its truth. What is born from this fusion, this Sacred Marriage of all the "separate" powers of heart, mind, body, and soul is the Sacred Androgyne, the one who in his or her being realizes the total interpenetration with the Christ of all normally "opposed" or "contradictory" qualities. This Sacred Androgyne—birthed in what early Gnostic writings such as the Gospel of Philip and the Acts of Thomas call again and again the "bridal Chamber," the place of fusion between "male" and "female"—is a divinized human divine being free of all normal categories of "male" and "female" because it exists in a unity that contains, absorbs, "uses," and ecstatically transcends both.... This Sacred Androgyne ... is the new Eve-Adam reuniting in his-her own being the Adam and Eve that we separated at the "Fall." In such a being, "heaven" lives on earth: through such a being the divine radiates divine grace and power directly.[11]

David White, a scholar of medieval Indian religion, takes this idea in a direction quite in line with my own:

Here [in the subtle body] all humans were viewed as essentially androgynous with sexual intercourse an affair between the female serpentine nexus of energy, generally called the *kundalini*, and a male principle, identified with Shiva, both of which were located in the subtle body.[12]

The "subtle body" refers to that dimension of awareness that embraces the physical in the spiritual. It is the place of ecstasy where the union of opposites takes place, or, more accurately, the always unified opposites are revealed as such. This is your own personal pilgrimage to the Holy of Holies, seeing the unity of masculine and feminine in the sacred sexual union of the two cherubim.

Again, there is no process of unification since the interbeing of all being is a given. What there is, and what the Song of Songs celebrates and awakens us to, is the unification that is an ever-present but oft overlooked reality.

To understand the deepest meaning of the Song of Songs, we have to move beyond its heterosexual trope and into the larger realm of what might be called polymorphous perversity.

Sigmund Freud coined the term "polymorphous perversity" in his discussion of infant sexuality. It means that one's entire body is open to pleasure and delight, and not simply those parts of the body sanctioned for such delight by adult society.

Thus Freud's doctrine of infantile sexuality, rightly understood, is essentially a scientific reformulation and reaffirmation of the religious and poetical theme of the innocence of childhood.... Freud takes with absolute seriousness the proposition of Jesus: "Except ye become as little children, ye can in no wise enter the kingdom of heaven." As a religious ideal, the innocence of childhood has turned out to resist assimilation into the rational-theological tradition. Only mystics and heretics like St. Francis and Jacob Boehme have made Christ's ideal their own. Poets like Blake and

Rilke have affirmed its secular validity. Rousseau attempted to grasp it in philosophic-rational terms. Freud formulated it as an indispensable axiom of scientific psychology.[13]

I am proposing this as an achievable state through sexual ecstasy as well. The body we are talking about isn't male or female; the sex we are talking about isn't straight or gay. We are simply using the bodies we see to realize the greater body we don't see.

Baruch Spinoza, the seventeenth-century Jewish philosopher, argues that enhancing the body enhances consciousness as well and longs for a "body fitted for many things."

Spinoza recognizes the "body fitted for many things" as the bodily counterpart of the intellectual love of God: "He who possesses a body fitted for doing many things, possesses the power of causing all the modifications of the body to be related to the idea of God, in consequence of which he is affected with a love of God which must occupy or form the greatest part of his mind, and therefore he possesses a mind of which the greatest part is eternal." Spinoza's intellectual love of God is identical with Freud's polymorphous perversity of children.[14]

This understanding of Spinoza, Freud, and polymorphous perversity is simply another way of saying what Job said millennia ago: "By means of my flesh I see God" (Job 19:26).

Sacred Sex

The Song of Songs, as I am reading it here, is a celebration of sacred sexuality: the union of the human seeker, represented by the male lover, with divine Wisdom, the Woman of Wholeness and Peace. The heterosexual trope of the Song of Songs is a product of its time and should not be mistaken as a limitation on who can partake of this mystery of union. Despite this, however, as a reader you will have to deal with the limits of language and transcend them for yourself.

Whenever the sex act is performed with holiness, with God being present, then there is a reenactment of the creation of the first couple. That is why in our Jewish wedding service, the liturgy says, "May You cause the bride and groom to rejoice as You did in Your creation in the primeval Garden of Eden."[15]

Neither Genesis nor the Song of Songs makes any mention of bride and groom. They speak of female and male, woman and man. The relationship between the lovers in both books is outside any formal marriage contract. So let us not impose a marriage where none exists and simply affirm that "when a man and a woman truly unite, all is one body and the cosmos rejoices for it becomes one complete corpus."[16]

I would go one step further and say that whenever two people, regardless of gender, "truly unite," they, too, become a single body and in so doing participate in the singularity, or non-duality, that is Ultimate Reality itself. Doing so is Wisdom, and embracing Wisdom is seeing God through one's flesh.

Scripture considers the sexual experience as knowledge; sexual experience coupled with love and desire will penetrate not only the mystery of sexuality but inevitably will draw one into the mysteries of existence.[17]

The key here is what it means to "truly unite." According to Jewish scholar Byron Sherwin, "For the Jewish mystics, the procreative act is a paradigm of the ultimate religious experience."[18] I would amend this slightly and say that sexual union as an expression of religiosity becomes a means for the ultimate religious experience. Intention is essential. If you embrace your partner for physical pleasure alone you may well miss the sacred dimension such union offers.

Adam and Eve, the first to be created, were originally one. Now they are two. They try to restore the status of old. Male and female are essentially part of a single whole. And though two bodies were separated, the two half-bodies are in constant search for each other. There will never be complete fulfillment until the male and the female are rejoined in a new unity.[19]

What is true of Adam and Eve is true of you and your partner, and true of the lovers in the Song of Songs as well. We are all originally one, and while we are still in fact one, we have allowed ourselves to be deluded by the illusion of separation. In reality there is no separation, but the union has to be lived in order to break through the illusion. One way to do this is through intentionally sacred sex: "Adam and Eve were one person. Through coupling they attained fulfillment, and when united face to face they symbolize completion of the divine structure."[20]

At the most heightened state of consciousness, the mystical experience has been perceived as an encounter between two intangible entities, namely the human soul and the Divine Reality. In order to express the abstract encounter therefore, the concrete has to be expediently employed. In this context, the paradigms of love between man and woman, in all its myriad aspects, have most often been employed by mystics as a means of expressing this experience.[21]

Sacred Love Stories

The Song of Songs is part of a genre of sacred love stories found in other religious traditions. Three in particular are worthy of mention here: the Islamic *Story of Layla and Majnun*, and the Hindu *Rasa-Lila* and *Gita Govinda*.

In diverse mystical traditions this ontological experience has been given emphasis because mystical union is arrived at only through the stages of a long and arduous path. This path, or journey, is expressed by the portrayal of human love-in-separation, in which the lovers are "torn" from each other. The separation is characterized by a searching, or quest, an intense longing. This state of affairs symbolizes the consciousness of the human soul of its separation from God, and a yearning to return to its Source.[22]

The Islamic *Story of Layla and Majnun* is based on an ancient Arabic poem describing the love between Qays and Layla. In what is perhaps its most famous version, composed by the Persian poet Nizami in the twelfth century, Qays and Layla meet and fall in love as students but cannot marry due to a feud between their two families. Qays composes poem after poem to express his love of Layla, and so all-consuming is his passion that the villagers give him the title *Majnun*, "The Possessed."

To keep the two lovers apart, Layla's father marries her off to another man, and she moves with her husband to northern Arabia where, perhaps like our Lady in the Song of Songs and Shakespeare's Juliet, she becomes sick with longing and dies. For his part Qays, shattered by the marriage of Layla to another man, flees into the desert to find his beloved. In time, Qays finds the grave of Layla and, after many adventures, dies nearby.

While there is no evidence that Nizami based his version of Layla and Majnun on the Song of Songs, it is interesting to note that Layla, like the Lady of the Song, is associated with a garden:

She was the most beautiful garden and Majnum was a torch of longing. She planted the rose-bush; he watered it with his tears.[23]

While the *Story of Layla and Majnun* has been read allegorically to describe the all-consuming love of the seeker for God, the story differs from the Song of Songs in one very important respect: unlike the man and woman of the Song, Qays and Layla never consummate their love. Theirs is a longing for union that is never realized.

Two examples of sacred love songs from India are the *Rasa-Lila* and the *Gita Govinda*.

Rasa-Lila, best translated as the Dance (*Lila*) of Divine Love (*Rasa*), was composed sometime in the second half of the first millennium CE as part of a larger work called the Bhagavata Purana and is often referred to as the Hindu "Song of Songs."[24] In a statement reminiscent of Rabbi Akiva's praise of the Song of Songs as the Holy of Holies, Hindu devotees of Vishnu, who they believe appears in the *Rasa-Lila* in the form of Krishna, celebrate the Bhagavata Purana as the essence of Hindu philosophy, and the *Rasa-Lila* as the essence of the Bhagavata Purana.[25]

The essence they refer to is the union of Atman with Brahman, the soul with God. While non-dualistic in its intent, and hence positing an eternal union of Atman and Brahman, the *Rasa-Lila* in particular and the Bhagavata Purana in general use the longing of the lover for the beloved as the central metaphor for spiritual awakening. Because the non-dual position is one of both/and rather than either/or, refusing to limit one to either the language of union or the language of separation, texts such as the Song of Songs, the *Rasa-Lila* , and the *Story of Layla and Majnun* can point toward the realization of non-duality within the metaphor of the union of opposites: lover and Beloved.

The *Gita Govinda*, or *Song of Govinda*, composed in the twelfth century by the Sanskrit poet Jayadeva, is another Indian love poem with spiritual implications. The *Gita Govinda* tells the story of Govinda, an incarnation of Lord Krishna, and his love for Radha, a milkmaid.

The parallels with the Song of Songs are not hard to find:

> She is visibly excited by embracing Hari [Lord Krishna];
> Her necklaces tremble on full, hard breasts....
> She is weary from ardently drinking his lips....
> Quivering earrings graze her cheeks;
> Her belt sounds with her hips' rolling motion.[26]

Like the Song of Songs and *Layla and Majnun*, in the *Gita Govinda* "the garden is central to the rich imagery of wild nature.... The lush natural surroundings convey the sense of pleasure the lovers have in each other."[27]

In this context gardens function symbolically in referring to particular existential realities, the earthly gardens signifying a worldly reality, which in turn signify a Divine Reality. In other words, the "real," earthly gardens have a relative reality, and the sacred gardens, an absolute Reality. The connection of the gardens, as the setting of the love stories, with the religious dimension, is thus apparent: it represents a refuge from the world.... Furthermore, in many Eastern cultures, the garden is a sexual symbol and a metaphor for woman's sexual arousal and desire ... particularly in the Song of Songs.[28]

My point in mentioning these other sacred love songs is to make clear that the Song of Songs is not unique and is in fact part of a genre of songs used as lenses through which we can see the union of lover and Beloved, seeker and God or God's Wisdom. But what are we to do with these songs? Are they simply poetic artifacts to be appreciated, or can they be lived in our own bodies?

If the former only, I would not find the Song of Songs as compelling as I do. It has to be embodied, just as the Beloved has to be embraced. "This love of the divine couple becomes a song, as well as a dance, and the reader is invited to join the celebration."[29]

For me the Song of Songs offers us a means by which to reunite *ish* and *ishah* to once again become *adam*, and in so doing reenter the Garden of Eden through the Garden that is the Beloved, Wisdom. "In other words, the Song of Songs redeems a love story gone awry."[30]

In the Genesis story we learn that the woman's desire is for the man, and that the man shall rule over her (3:16). But in the Song of Songs "there is no male dominance, no female subordination, and no stereotyping of either sex."[31]

Male and female first became one flesh in the garden of Eden. There a narrator reported briefly their sexual union (Genesis 2:24). Now in another garden, the lovers themselves praise at length the joys of intercourse. Possessive adjectives do not separate their lives. "My garden" and "his garden" blend in mutual

habitation and harmony. Even person and place unite: the garden of eroticism is the woman.[32]

The meaning I offer in this book is not the final one, but it is a powerful one. I encourage you not only to read the Song of Songs but also to
experiment with it; not only to envision the imagery but also to embody
it; not only to celebrate the love of Wisdom and seeker but also to realize
it in your own flesh.

Song of Songs

1 The doubling of "songs" (*Shir haShirim* in Hebrew) implies the importance of this poem. This is the most important of all songs, the greatest of all poems.

2 The additional phrase "by Solomon" (*asher liShlomo*) could render this verse as "the greatest of all Solomon's songs." According to 1 Kings 5:12, Solomon authored 1,005 poems and songs, so the Song of Songs might be one of them, and the best one at that. Most likely, however, the reference to King Solomon isn't historical. By linking the Song of Songs to Solomon, the poet was engaging in pseudepigrapha, ascribing one's work to that of a well-known and long-dead person to guarantee the book a wider audience.

☐ Chapter One

1:1
The Song of Songs,[1] by Solomon.[2]

(continued on page 59)

3 The Song opens with a fully sexualized yearning. Wisdom wants your mouth on her mouth. From the very first moments of your birth, your mouth was a gateway to intimacy and knowing. Wisdom invites you to reclaim that early innocence. Knowing in this sense is not abstract or intellectual. In Hebrew, *yada*, "to know," is often a euphemism for sexual union. The knowing Wisdom offers is deeply intimate. Uniting with Wisdom frees you from the illusion of being apart from Ultimate Reality and awakens you to the ecstasy and joy of being a part of it.

4 This may refer to the perfumed oils the ancients rubbed onto their bodies and hair and also to the oils secreted by your body in moments of intense passion.

5 Wisdom delights in humankind (Proverbs 8:31) and perhaps desires you more than you desire her, so much so that even thinking about you arouses her.

6 Wisdom is not the only one who seeks you, however. Life is filled with distractions. But these are "young women," unripe passions, well-packaged but false opinions and theories. Wisdom is ancient and timeless. She is the first of God's creations (Proverbs 8:22) and yet as fresh as this very instant. With her alone can you find truth and liberation.

7 Where is your secret place? Where do you go to escape the unripe passions and surrender to the Unknown—truth so raw that it cannot be bound up in words? This is where Wisdom is met.

8 The Song grounds the spiritual in the physical. As Job says, "Through my flesh I see God" (Job 19:26). Wisdom isn't spiritual in opposition to material, or otherworldly in opposition to this world. Wisdom is the Tao, the way of all being and becoming.

Wisdom Speaks

1:2
Kiss me! Your mouth on mine!
Your love is more intoxicating than wine.[3]

1:3
Your skin yields fragrant oil[4]
the very thought of you
releases my own perfume.[5]
No wonder young women crave you![6]

1:4
Quickly!
Pull me into your secret place.[7]
Let us grow wild in one another,
drunk on love's wine.[8]
Young women are right to desire you!

(continued on page 61)

9 | Wisdom is black, as in deep, mysterious. She is the Dark Female of the Tao Te Ching (chapter 6). She is the Hindu Black Mother Kali, whose love slays the illusions under which you live, allowing you to awaken to truth. She is the Black Madonna, the deepest womb from which emerges the Christ, the consciousness that knows its unity with the One.

10 | While Kedar was a city known for its riches (see Isaiah 21:16; Jeremiah 49:28–29; Ezekiel 27:21), the word *kedar* is probably also a play on the Hebrew *k-d-r*, "to be dark or black," emphasizing the mysterious nature of Wisdom.

11 | The Hebrew here is *yeri'ot* and may mean "curtains." In Jeremiah 49:28–29, we are told that the *yeri'ot* of Kedar are among the prized objects looted from the city.

12 | Here are the twin dangers of gazing upon the Dark Female: entrapment and fear. Rather than daring to know the mystery, you become entrapped in the fantasies you spin about mystery. Fearing you will become lost in her mystery, you seek to control her rather than surrender to her.

13 | Wisdom's brothers are actually her half-brothers, "sons of my mother." Her half-brothers are half-truths about reality rather than reality itself. Wisdom is warning you not to mistake the menu for the meal (Proverbs 9:2–6); not to force reality to fit your theories, but to drop all theories and perceive directly what is so.

14 | "Your flock" is the notions you nurture. On what are they nourished: on truth, on illusion? Where do they rest and become still, allowing your mind to cool and glimpse what is without the distractions of what you desire should be?

15 | "Your companions" parallel Wisdom's half-brothers: half-truths that walk with you in your travels. Prostitutes were known by their veils (Genesis 38:15). Must Wisdom veil herself and play the harlot, navigating among the illusions you treasure in order to find you? Or will you dare to meet her on her terms, unveiled and free?

1:5

I am black and beautiful,[9]
O daughters of Jerusalem.
Black as Kedar's goat-hair tents.[10]
Beautiful as Solomon's finest curtains.[11]

1:6

I am darker than sun-baked skin,
yet don't let my darkness entrap you.
My mother's sons feared me[12]
and forced me to tend their vineyards,
while my own vineyard I could not tend![13]

1:7

Tell me, my true love,
you for whom my breath pants,
where does your flock graze?
Where do they lay down at noon?[14]
Must I wander as a whore
veiled among the flocks of your companions?[15]

(continued on page 63)

16 If you could step away from your flock, if you could meet Wisdom without illusion, you would, but you can't. So you beg Wisdom to track your illusions and, in this way, find you among them and lead you out of them toward Truth.

17 Horses are often used in the Hebrew Bible as symbols of wealth and sometimes lust (Deuteronomy 17:16–17; Isaiah 2:7–8; Jeremiah 5:8; Ezekiel 23:20). Your yearning for Wisdom is powerful, but not powerful enough to draw you away from your flocks, your touchstones of certainty and security. You need Wisdom to find you (see Proverbs 1:20, 8:1–2, 9:3), for only then can you leave your path and enter her mysteries.

18 In this verse you call Wisdom your "friend," just as she will call you friend in Song 5:16. Your relationship is not only intimate but also equal: you are one another's friend. The book of Ecclesiastes, also attributed to King Solomon, celebrates friendship and urges you to find a beloved friend with whom to share your work, your trials, and your bed (Ecclesiastes 4:9–11).

19 The Hebrew here is *torim*, and its meaning is unknown. The root word of *torim* is *t-w-r*, which means "to circle," so I imagine *torim* are hooped earrings.

20 While it is natural to adorn Wisdom with what you consider valuable, Wisdom herself is more valuable than even the most priceless pearl (Proverbs 8:11). You need add nothing to Wisdom, for her beauty is complete.

The Seeker Responds

1:8
If you don't know, my fairest,
follow the tracks of the flock,
and graze your goats in the cooler grass
beside my shepherds' tents.[16]

1:9
Like a mare among Pharaoh's stallions,[17]
you compel me to you, my friend.[18]

1:10
Your cheeks offset with hooped earrings,[19]
your neck encircled with jewels.

1:11
I will make you earrings of gold studded with silver.[20]

(continued on page 65)

21 The reference to the seeker as "king" is another example of why some commentators imagine the Song of Songs to be about King Solomon. I suggest this is merely a term of endearment.

22 Ein Gedi is an oasis in the Judean wilderness. The sweet spice smell of her lover is in rare contrast to the near odorless desert, and thus all the more intoxicating. Just as the woman calls her lover a cluster of blossoms in this verse, so he will call her a cluster of dates in Song 7:9.

The focus on smell in 1:12–14—the Beloved's scent of yearning, her lover's smell of henna—suggests the power of smell as an aphrodisiac. This is why I suggest using fragrant oils or incense, especially frankincense and myrrh, when reading the Song of Songs with a friend.

23 Nothing compares to Wisdom's beauty (see Proverbs 16:16).

24 Doves mate with only one lover; Wisdom's eyes are for you alone. Wisdom's eyes are described as doves in Song 4:1, and she describes your eyes as doves in 5:12.

25 While, as we shall see, these lovers are not averse to making love indoors, they also find great joy in making love outdoors in the green forests. Compare Wisdom's bed with that of Solomon's (Song 3:9–10). The bed of the powerful is an artifact designed to show off that power. The bed of Wisdom is nature. Where Solomon's bed is held up by cedars cut down and carved, Wisdom's beams are the living cedars themselves.

Wisdom Speaks

1:12
Lying with my king on his couch,
my body fills the air
with the scent of yearning.[21]

1:13
Lying between my breasts
My lover is fragrant as myrrh;
his spice intoxicates me,

1:14
like a fragrant cluster of henna blossoms from Ein Gedi.[22]

The Seeker Speaks

1:15
Your beauty, my love,
is beyond anything we call beautiful![23]
Your eyes are doves.[24]

1:16
You are beautiful, my beloved,
truly lovely.
Our bed is green grass;

1:17
cedar trees are our bedroom's beams;
and pine its rafters.[25]

1 The Hebrew prophets mention these two plants, the rose (*chavatze-let*) and the lily (*shoshanah*) as signs of redemption: "The wilderness shall rejoice and bloom like a *chavatzelet*" (Isaiah 35:1), and Israel "shall blossom as the *shoshanah*" (Hosea 14:6). The Hosea passage is especially telling. In it God says, "I will love them [the people Israel] gratuitously" (Hosea 14:5, ArtScroll Stone translation). Gratuitous love is love without cause or reason. God will love the people regardless of their history. The Song evokes this sense of limitless, gratuitous love with the choice of these flowers. The rose of Sharon and the lilies of the valley are wild, not sown and cultivated. They are not grown to be sold but appear naturally of their own accord. Wisdom is saying, "I am the child of God's infinite love, and my love is a freely given gift to those I choose to love." In other words, you cannot earn or merit Wisdom, you can only learn to heed her call.

This is what Jesus says when he, too, uses lilies as symbols of a life lived in complete trust without an hour's worth of worry (Matthew 6:27–28). Living this way is not living without labor, but it is living without coercion. This is what the Taoists call *wei wu wei*, acting by not acting, or non-coercive action. This is swimming with the current, cutting with the grain. Wisdom is the one who teaches you the current and grain of life. Acting in accord with her is living wisely and well.

☐ Chapter Two

Wisdom Speaks

2:1
I am a rose of Sharon,
a wild lily of the valleys.[1]

(*continued on page 69*)

2   Here the seeker recognizes Wisdom's beauty to be so startling as to reduce all other beautiful things to mere brambles. "Wisdom is more precious than rubies, and nothing you desire can compare with her" (Proverbs 3:15, 8:11). "Coral and jasper are not worthy of mention; the value of wisdom is beyond rubies" (Job 28:18).

Now ask yourself: what do you value beyond everything else? Is it Wisdom or something less? Most of us value something less, something we can tame, something we can use for our own ends. Something we can employ to bend the world to our will. But Wisdom is not about bending the world to our will, but about bending our will to the world. Wisdom isn't about making things go the way we want, but about learning how to navigate the world the way it is. Loving Wisdom and living wisely require great skill and non-coercive action.

Wisdom is beyond any price, and thus the cost to you is everything you treasure. Until you have given all for Wisdom—until you are emptied of every idea, dream, fantasy, and ideology—you cannot receive her.

The Seeker Responds

2:2
A lily among brambles, my love,
a gorgeous flower among
the thicket of young maidens.[2]

(continued on page 71)

3 Many translations render *tappuach* as "apple," but apples are not native to the region. Along with others, I identify *tappuach* with apricots, a fruit that is both native and common.

4 Wisdom lingers: she is in no hurry to bring your meeting to a climax or an end. Union with Wisdom takes time and, as she admonishes the daughters of Jerusalem over and again, must not be rushed (see Song 2:7, 3:5, 8:4).

5 Wisdom lingers in your shade, meaning that you are standing over her. This is not a position of dominance, however. On the contrary, you are yielding your body to her.

6 The image of Lady Wisdom orally pleasuring your genitals is a counterpart to your kissing her mouth in Song 1:2. The oral nature of the intimacy is key; she is knowing you in the most primal way we humans know: through the mouth.

In the kabbalistic Tree of Life, the genitals are linked to the *sefirah* of *Yesod*, Foundation, where the physical and spiritual dimensions of reality are intertwined like yin and yang. This is also the place of coiled-serpent Kundalini, the energy that rises through the body as it awakens its true nature as a manifestation of Ultimate Reality.

7 The Hebrew here is *beit ha-yayin*, literally "the wine house." Some take this to be a "pub" or "banquet hall," but Wisdom isn't an exhibitionist, and it makes no sense that she wishes to make love with you in public. In fact, she tells us that while she would like to kiss you in public as if you were her brother, you aren't and she can't (Song 8:1). Rather than pull you into a public space, she draws you from the vineyard into the winepress, a more secluded spot where she can give herself to you in private.

Wisdom Speaks

2:13
And you, my love,
stand out among the young men
as an apricot tree stands out in a forest.[3]
I linger[4] in your shade,[5]
your fruit is sweet in my mouth.[6]

2:4
Bring me to the winepress,
and enfold me with love.[7]

(continued on page 73)

8 Wisdom's desire for you is overwhelming and threatens to weaken her to the point of fainting. The cake and fruit, probably not metaphorical, are meant to keep you embodied and not let your passion abandon the physical even as it lifts the physical into the spiritual.

9 This is a recurring refrain in the Song, making your physical embrace of Wisdom explicit. The mention of both left and right hands speaks to the unity of opposites that union with Wisdom entails. The left hand symbolizes intuition; the right hand symbolizes reason. Wisdom is not one or the other, or one at the expense of the other, but both.

10 The daughters of Jerusalem are probably a women's chorus, suggesting that the Song of Songs was performed. In our reading they are also the apostles of Lady Wisdom, whom she sends into the world to draw humanity to her (Proverbs 9:3).

11 Union with Wisdom is as natural to humans as mating is to gazelles or wild deer. This is not a supernatural or disembodied union, but a natural and fully physical one.

12 The daughters of Jerusalem seem not to understand the way Wisdom works. Wisdom worries that they will mistake one level of sexual completion for the fully completed love that Wisdom offers. While Wisdom embraces your body, she is not content with your body alone. There is more ripening to follow, and this cannot be rushed. What looks like completion may not be, and you must be willing to see the union through to the end, to not be distracted by anything less than full awakening, no matter how rare and exquisite.

2:5
Sustain me with raisin cakes;
refresh me with apricots;
I am feverish with love.[8]

2:6
I yearn for your left hand beneath my head,
your right hand pulling me to you![9]

2:7
Swear to me, daughters of Jerusalem,[10]
as you would not disturb mating gazelles or wild deer:[11]
do not disturb our lovemaking until we are through![12]

(continued on page 75)

13 While some translators put the lovers at a distance from one another in this verse, given the physical intimacy they are already sharing, doing so makes little sense. What Wisdom hears is your soft groaning of desire as you move your mouth over her body from the mountains of her pubic area (mons pubis) and belly to the hills of her breasts. This parallels her pleasuring you in Song 2:3 and again speaks to the slow raising of the Kundalini from the base of the spine through the top of the head.

14 Placing the lover behind a wall separating Wisdom and the seeker makes no sense. The seeker is moving his mouth up from her genitals to her mouth. The "wall" they share (*katleinu*, "our wall") is their flesh. You are gazing into Wisdom's eyes ("windows"), half-closed in the throes of passion, and she sees you through the lattice of her lashes.

15 Embraced in one another's arms, Wisdom hears you whispering in her ear urging her to join you in a shared moment of ecstasy.

16 These are all images of ripening, euphemisms of pending sexual release.

17 Again you urge Wisdom to join you in ecstasy. It is important that you experience this ecstasy together. Wisdom is not a passive force transmitting theories, but a dynamic force revealing what is only when you unite with her in mutual longing and love.

2:8
I hear my lover's voice,
his breath panting upon my mountains,
bounding over my hills.¹³

2:9
You are like a gazelle—
a young stag!
I see you standing behind our wall,
gazing in at the windows,
looking through the lattice.¹⁴

2:10
I hear you whispering to me:
"Awake, my love, my beauty,
and come away with me.¹⁵

2:11
The winter is past,
and with it the rains.

2:12
Wildflowers brighten the earth;
birdsong rides the air,
and the meadows ring with the cooing of turtledoves.

2:13
The fig trees sprout,
and the grapevines bloom;
and their spice defines the air.¹⁶
Quickly, my love, my fair one, come away.¹⁷

(continued on page 77)

18 You want to hear Wisdom moaning with passion, as she has heard
you do the same. You long to see her face abandoned to ecstasy. Wisdom desires you no less than you desire her. But this is often difficult
to accept; you feel unworthy of her love. Seeing her desire for you
allows you to overcome self-doubt and surrender to her.

19 The seeker is addressing an audience here, most likely the daughters
of Jerusalem, the only people mentioned thus far in the Song of Songs.
Just as Wisdom commanded them not to disturb their lovemaking, so
you entreat them to catch and hold anything that would ruin the per-
fection of this moment.

20 This is the moment of orgasmic union dissolving any separation
between Wisdom and seeker, Beloved and lover.

21 Wisdom gives herself to those capable of feeding among her lilies,
the symbol of wild, gratuitous love. Wisdom cannot be bought or con-
trolled, and only when you drop any desire for either can your desire
for Wisdom be consummated.

22 Just as Wisdom herself is dark (Song 1:5), so union with her takes
place in the dark. The Song isn't speaking only of night and day, but of
the hidden and the revealed, the unknown and the known. If you wish
to unite with Wisdom, you must abandon all illusion and then enter
into the dark unknown that is Wisdom herself.

23 In Song 4:6, Wisdom's body is compared to mountains of myrrh and
frankincense. Here Wisdom is urging you to embrace her completely.

2:14
O my dove, in the clefts of the rock,
in the shadows of the cliff,
let me see your face,
let me hear your voice;
your voice is enchanting,
and your face is stunning.[18]

2:15
Catch us the foxes,
the little foxes that ruin the vineyards—
for our vineyards are in blossom."[19]

2:16
My beloved is mine and I am his[20]
feeding among the lilies.[21]

2:17
Before the dawn sighs
and night's shadows flee,
encircle me, my beloved,[22]
like a gazelle or a young stag
on the mountains of spice.[23]

1 Wisdom has a recurring dream in which she seeks you and cannot find you. She calls to you, and yet you don't respond. Why not? Ask yourself, "What is making me deaf to Wisdom? What keeps me from responding to her call?"

2 In the book of Proverbs, Wisdom calls to you in the streets of the city (8:1–6); she does the same in her dream. Why can't she find you? Where are you hiding? Why are you hiding?

3 The city guards protect the status quo: the official creeds, dogma, doctrines, and institutions that determine what is allowed and normative. Wisdom calls you to step beyond all these. Wisdom asks if the guards know your whereabouts—she wonders if you are under their protection, if you are caught in the official truths and hence incapable of Wisdom. They, like you, don't respond to her questions. Is this because they don't want to give you up? Or is it because you are hiding elsewhere?

☐ Chapter Three

Wisdom Speaks

3:1
Night after night in my bed
I seek you, my love;
I seek you, but I can't find you;
I call you, but you don't reply.[1]

3:2
So I say to myself,
> "I will leave my bed and wander the city,
> searching street and square for you
> for whom my breath pants."
So I sought you, but could not find you.[2]

3:3
But I was found,
the city guards came upon me during their rounds.
"Have you seen my beloved?" I ask them,
[but they too don't reply.][3]

(continued on page 81)

4 As soon as Wisdom moves beyond the guards, she finds you. You aren't a prisoner of the guards, nor do they protect you. They merely stand between you and Wisdom. You could not cross them, so you wait until Wisdom passes by them. You want to be found but lack the courage to step into the open. So conditioned are we by the guardians of truth that even when we know their truths to be mere opinion, still we are frozen in place. Just as Wisdom is unguarded, so you must be unguarded. Whatever you cling to, whatever creeds and isms and ideologies define you, you must drop them all if Wisdom is to be your love.

5 Making love on one's mother's bed is first found in Genesis 24:67, when Isaac takes Rebecca into his mother's tent to make love with her. In the Song of Songs, Wisdom leads you into her mother's house, indeed onto her mother's bed, deeper into the feminine mysteries, the dark interior where all opposites unite and where Wisdom and the seeker of Wisdom become one. Wisdom's Mother is *YHVH* (Proverbs 8:22), the Unknown and Unknowable Is-ing that gives rise to all things.

6 The daughters of Jerusalem parallel the city guards. Where the guards represent the status quo, the official truths supported by the powers that be, the daughters represent the not yet realized unripe wisdom. Both must be overcome. You must dare to step away from the isms and ideologies considered normative and be willing to be led by Wisdom deeper into the feminine dimension of relationship and union. You must steel yourself against the siren song of the daughters, the pleasurable distractions that keep you from going deeper still. The ripening of Wisdom takes time. You must learn to trust the process and settle for nothing less than the all-consuming love Wisdom promises.

3:4
Scarcely had I left them,
that I found you, my love.[4]
I grasp you to me,
and pull you into my mother's house,
into her bedchamber
and onto the very bed on which I was conceived.[5]

3:5
Swear to me, daughters of Jerusalem,
as you would not disturb mating gazelles or wild deer:
do not disturb our lovemaking until we are through![6]

(continued on page 83)

7 In her dream Wisdom has found you and led you onto her mother's bed to make love with you. She has just urged the daughters of Jerusalem not to disturb you, when they are immediately distracted by some disturbance in the desert.

The daughters are seduced by the romance of exotic incense and caravan spices and hope to distract you from Wisdom by drawing your attention to these.

8 The irony here is that while Wisdom calls and you remain silent, the daughters of Jerusalem and the city guards are all too willing to talk. They are the chatter in your head that keeps you distracted from Wisdom. But the chatter of the daughters and the chatter of the guards are of two different types. Where the daughters speak of the romantic, the ethereal, and the exotic, the guards speak of power, solidity, and even violence.

Where the daughters of Jerusalem see a caravan of blowing spice, the guards see the litter of a warrior king. Where Wisdom's bed is unguarded, warriors surround the bed imagined by the guards, men more powerful even than themselves. Where Wisdom's bed is for lovemaking, the bed these men see is a place of battle. It is important to note that while the bed is said to belong to Solomon, and the city's guards call the daughters of Jerusalem to "gaze upon King Solomon" (Song 3:11), we never actually see him at all.

9 Wisdom's dream paints a portrait of opposites, all of which must be overcome. If you would find ecstasy in her bed, the beds of romance or power must not distract you.

The Daughters of Jerusalem Inquire

3:6
Who is this coming up from the wilderness,
stirring the sands like clouds of incense,
perfuming the air with a caravan's
powders, spices, and herbs?[7]

The City Guards Respond

3:7
Look, it's the bed of Solomon[8]
surrounded by sixty great warriors of Israel,

3:8
battle hardened
and each with a sword strapped to his thigh
to defend against attackers in the night.[9]

(continued on page 85)

10 Compare Wisdom's bed to Solomon's. Where Wisdom's bed is natural—green grass and trees of pine and cedar (Song 1:16–17)—Solomon's bed is an artifact, nature coerced into furniture. The city guards are enthralled by power, just as the daughters are enthralled by romance. Wisdom's dream warns you to avoid both.

11 Just as Wisdom tended her half-brothers' vineyards (Song 1:6), so the daughters of Jerusalem upholstered Solomon's bed. The difference is that Wisdom breaks free of her half-brothers, while the daughters remain enthralled to romance.

12 The city guards invite the daughters of Jerusalem to share in their vision of male power rather than the female mystery Wisdom herself offers. This is the opposite of Wisdom's female apostles, who scour the cities calling humanity to Wisdom's feast (Proverbs 9:3–6).

13 This is the second "mother" mentioned in the Song of Songs. The first was Wisdom's mother, *YHVH*, the Tao that cannot be named and yet is called the Great Mother (Tao Te Ching, chapter 6). Solomon's mother is the place from which power arises.

14 This is the first mention of a wedding. Solomon, symbolizing power and order, must be married; his union must be within the norms of the state. Wisdom is unmarried, and there is no wedding of Wisdom with the seeker of Wisdom. Her love and her lovemaking are outside the strictures of society. Wisdom is untamed and free; Solomon, for all his power, is constrained. Indeed, it may be his power that constrains him.

3:9
Its bedframe is Lebanon's cedars.

3:10
Its posts are silver,
its floor is gold,
its mattresses wrapped in purple;
and its interior lovingly inlaid by Jerusalem's daughters.[10, 11]

3:11
Come out, O daughters of Zion,
and gaze upon King Solomon,[12]
crowned by his mother[13] on the day of his wedding,[14]
the day of his heart's rejoicing.

1 Wisdom's dream is over, and in this chapter we find the lovers in each other's embrace. Where the daughters of Jerusalem spoke in the language of mystery, and the city guards spoke in the language of power, the seeker speaks in the language of nature.

2 When Wisdom spoke of wearing a veil, she did so in reference to prostitution (Song 1:7). When you speak of the veil, it is in reference to the alluring nature of Wisdom's beauty. The veil here may also be symbolic. Saint Paul teaches that you cannot know Wisdom except through a glass, darkly (1 Corinthians 13:12), and the Talmudic Rabbis say that even the prophets saw God "through a dark and lightless lens" (Babylonian Talmud, *Yevamot* 49b). The Song may be saying that even when only a veil separates you from Wisdom, even that is too much.

3 This reference to David's tower and battlements hearkens back to the city guards' vision of Solomon's bed surrounded by warriors ready for battle. But there is a difference. Where Solomon's soldiers battle for power, Wisdom, like the Hindu goddess Kali whose neck is adorned by the skulls of the illusions she has killed, wears a garland of shields once owned by the falsehoods she has overcome. Both Wisdom and Kali destroy the illusions that keep you seeing reality as it is.

☐ Chapter Four

The Seeker Speaks

4:1
How gorgeous you are, my love,
how strikingly beautiful![1]
Your eyes are doves behind your veil.[2]
Your black hair ripples down your shoulders—
black goats streaming down the slopes of Gilead.

4:2
Your teeth are white and even—
a flock of shorn ewes
each with its twin coming up from washing.

4:3
Your lips are a crimson thread,
and your mouth so inviting.
Your cheeks curve like pomegranate halves
behind your veil.

4:4
Your neck is strong and
straight as David's tower
adorned with a thousand shields.[3]

(continued on page 89)

4 Again the intimacy of lover and Beloved takes place at night. Wisdom is a kind of knowing that happens only when you dare to enter the dark, the unknown. Wisdom is the Dark Lady (Song 1:5) and must be met in the darkness of unknowing.

5 With this verse a new name is given the Beloved: bride. This is a powerful title but not a legal one. No marriage has taken place. Beloved and lover are not wife and husband in the eyes of some external authority—the city guards, for example. Rather, calling Wisdom your bride binds you to her exclusively. Your love of Wisdom is absolute, and no other will lure you away.

6 The necklace of Wisdom, similar to that of Mother Kali, is made up of the shields of the defeated illusions and delusions that have kept you from her. Remember, the price of Wisdom is surrendering all you think you know; the death of all to which you cling. Just seeing this necklace deepens your liberation.

7 Now a third title is offered: sister. Together these three titles—beloved, bride, and sister—represent the three ways in which your love of Wisdom must manifest: Beloved represents ecstasy. Bride represents trustworthiness. Sister represents friendship.

4:5
Your two breasts are fawns,
twins of a gazelle
feeding among the lilies.

4:6
Until the day dawns
and the shadows flee,
I will climb your mountain of myrrh
and hill of frankincense.[4]

4:7
You are altogether beautiful,
my flawless love.

4:8
Come with me from Lebanon, my bride;[5]
come down from the high peaks,
and depart the dens of mountain leopard and lion.

4:9
A single glance,
a mere twinkling of your necklace,[6]
and my heart is raptured, my sister, my bride.[7]

(continued on page 91)

8 While some translators speak of the scent of the woman's garments, my own reading is that the lovers are naked and the only thing "covering" the Beloved is her scent.

9 The scent of the cedars of Lebanon offers an alternative to the actual cedars used to make Solomon's bed. The cedars of the bed are cut down and dead, forced to fit the shape we imagine and not the shape nature intended for them. What counts is their massiveness, not their fragrance. With Wisdom, however, the forests are alive, and it is their fragrance that matters, not their material heaviness. The bed of Solomon is a symbol of power; the scent of cedar enveloping Wisdom is a return to nature and the natural ecstasy of love.

10 Wisdom calls to you from the mountain peaks and city squares, but she herself is private, hidden, and secluded. This is not a case of "many are called, but few are chosen" (Matthew 22:14), for Wisdom calls to all humanity, the wise and the foolish (Proverbs 1:20–21). There is no selection of an elect in the Song of Songs; Wisdom delights in all humankind (Proverbs 8:31). What the Song is saying is that while Wisdom calls to all of us, not everyone is willing to respond to her. Not everyone is willing to enter the dark place of unknowing, the private garden of ecstasy, the hidden well of understanding, the secluded fountain of her delights in which she is found.

4:10
My sister, my bride!
How intoxicating is your love!
I am drunk on the fragrance of your oil, your spice!

4:11
Your lips glisten with nectar, my bride;
honey and milk are under your tongue;
your scent is your only garment[8]—the scent of Lebanon's
forests.[9]

4:12
My sister, my bride,
you are a private garden,
a hidden well,
a secluded fountain.[10]

(continued on page 93)

11 These images from nature are metaphors, euphemisms for Wisdom's body yielding to yours in the heat of sexual union. Her private garden is her vagina. Her hidden well is the wetness of her passion. Her secluded fountain is the rush of her orgasm that flows powerfully like the streams of Lebanon.

12 The "winds" are not natural winds, for north winds and south winds cannot blow at the same time. The wind is your breath hovering over Wisdom's body from head to toe. It is this that excites her and causes her spices to flow as she becomes wet with desire.

13 Notice that Wisdom calls her garden "his garden" in this verse. This isn't to imply that she has abandoned her garden to you or that you have somehow forced her to tend your garden rather than her own, as did her half-brothers (Song 1:6). Rather it is that Wisdom is inviting you to a level of union that makes distinctions between you irrelevant. Wisdom invites you into her garden so deeply that you will imagine it to be your own.

4:13
Yet you extend your branches
like a pomegranate orchard
laden with fruit,
blossoming with henna and saffron,

4:14
with the incense of cinnamon, musk, myrrh, and aloes,
with the most precious spices and perfumes.

4:15
And within your garden a fountain,
a spring of living water
flowing like the streams of Lebanon.[11]

Wisdom Responds

4:16
O north wind!
O south wind!
Breathe upon my garden.
Let my spices flow![12]
Let my beloved come to his garden
and eat its choicest fruits.[13]

1 Just as Wisdom invited you to see her garden as your garden in the previous chapter, so here you accept that invitation, so intimately united with Wisdom that you see her body as your body and revel in her pleasure as your pleasure. This is not a statement of Wisdom's surrender or the seeker's dominance, and even less a patriarchal ownership of a woman's body. Rather this is a level of union so complete that pleasuring the other pleasures you.

2 Calling Wisdom sister-bride makes it clear that your union is more than a fleeting thing. This love manifests as physical ecstasy (beloved) but also as friendship (sister) and trustworthy devotion (bride). You must become not only Wisdom's lover, but her sibling and her spouse as well.

3 Just as Lady Wisdom ate the apricots of the seeker earlier (Song 2:3), here the seeker reciprocates and pleasures her orally as well.

4 Wine is a metaphor for passion (Song 1:2, 1:4), but Wisdom offers more than wine. She offers milk as well. While wine may lead us into the ecstasy of love, milk sustains us in the life that follows.

5 We have no idea who these "friends" may be. Are they the daughters of Jerusalem or the guardians of the city? Or perhaps "friends" is merely a way for the poet to urge all people to enter into the divine embrace of Wisdom.

6 To be drunk is to step beyond the distinctions of good and bad, female and male, right and wrong into the greater unity that Wisdom offers.

☐ Chapter Five

The Seeker Speaks

5:1
I enter my garden,[1] my sister, my bride;[2]
I gather my myrrh and my spice.
I eat my honeycomb dripping my honey.[3]
I drink my wine with my milk.[4]
Eat, friends,[5] and drink—get drunk on love.[6]

(continued on page 97)

7 Wisdom offers you a second dream. In the first (Song 3:1), she sought you but you did not respond. In the second, you seek her and she doesn't respond. In the earlier dream, you hesitated; in this dream, you are too eager. The way of Wisdom is "call and response"—you are called and must respond at the moment you are called. In this dream, you act prematurely, not waiting for her call but acting on your own desire.

8 This is clearly a euphemism. There is no reason why a dew-moistened head should lead Wisdom to open the door to her chamber and let you enter. The dew-moistened head refers to your being aroused for Wisdom even though she is not ready for you.

9 In Proverbs 9:1–6, Wisdom prepares her feast and invites you to her table only when she is ready. Here you knock uninvited. Just as the daughters of Jerusalem may be too eager to end your lovemaking, here you are too eager to begin. It is Lady Wisdom who determines the rightness of the moment for union.

10 The dream shifts from demanding entrance to invoking desire. The literal translation of this verse is "my beloved stretches his hand through the hole." There is a clear double entendre here. The lock in the dream is in reality Wisdom's vagina.

11 Wisdom is aroused, her feast is prepared, and she rises to unlock the door.

12 When she opens the door, however, you are gone. The meaning is about timing, moving slowly and not rushing into intimacy unprepared. The dream opens with the seeker rushing things; now it is Wisdom who finds that she has waited too long.

Wisdom Speaks

5:2
I slept, and my heart dreamed.
Listen! I heard you knocking, my beloved:[7]
> *"Open to me, my sister, my love,*
> *my dove, my perfect one;*
> *for my head is wet,*
> *my hair is damp with evening dew."*[8]

5:3
I had put off my garment;
how could I put it on again?
I had bathed my feet;
how could I soil them?[9]

5:4
You thrust your hand into the lock,
and my body ached for you.[10]

5:5
I arose to open to you, beloved,
my fingers wet with myrrh,
dripping my oil on the latch.[11]

5:6
I opened to you, my beloved,
but you were gone.
My breath failed me when you spoke.
I sought you, but did not find you;
I called you, but there was no reply.[12]

(continued on page 99)

13 The last time Wisdom met the city guards (Song 3:3), they ignored her; now they beat her and strip her of her clothes, which may be a euphemism for rape. Why the change? Perhaps the first time Wisdom was veiled (Song 1:7), and they mistook her for a prostitute and had no interest in her. This time there is no veil. Wisdom is seen for who she is: a threat to the guardians of power and the status quo.

14 Previously Wisdom called upon the daughters of Jerusalem to refrain from disturbing your lovemaking (Song 2:7); now she turns to her maidens to help her find you. In this the daughters of Jerusalem play the role of Lady Wisdom's apostles in Proverbs 9:3. They seek you out and call you to her.

15 In asking for details about her lover, the daughters of Jerusalem provide Wisdom with an opportunity to celebrate your body as you celebrated her body in chapter 4.

5:7

The city's guards found me on their rounds.

These watchmen beat me, wounded me,

and stripped me of my cloak.[13]

5:8

I beg you, daughters of Jerusalem,

if you find my beloved, tell him this:

I am feverish with love.[14]

The Daughters of Jerusalem Inquire

5:9

Describe him to us, Beautiful Woman.

How is your beloved superior to others?[15]

(continued on page 101)

16 What makes you stand out among the masses is a passion for life, suggesting that this is a prerequisite for finding Wisdom. Wisdom is not an ascetic pursuit, demanding renunciation of the material world or denigration of the physical. On the contrary, Wisdom rejoices in this world and delights in humankind (Proverbs 8:31). To attract Wisdom you must do the same.

17 Sapphires have special significance in the Hebrew Bible. In Exodus 24:10 sapphire represents "the essence of heaven in all its purity," and in Ezekiel 1:26 the prophet sees the sapphire throne of God. Being encrusted with sapphires may suggest that the seeker, to be worthy of Wisdom's love, must be pierced with the desire to know the Divine. If this is so, it is the yin to the red glow's yang. That is, you must be fully engaged with the world but in a manner that is pierced through with intimations of divinity. Union with Wisdom isn't physical or spiritual, but physical and spiritual.

Wisdom Responds

5:10
My beloved glows red with life,
a beacon among ten thousand.[16]

5:11
His skin the color of polished gold,
his hair wavy and raven black.

5:12
His eyes like doves resting in pools of milk.

5:13
His cheeks like spice beds,
his lips lilies glistening with myrrh.

5:14
His arms are rounded gold, set with jewels.
His stomach smooth and hard as ivory,
encrusted with sapphires.[17]

5:15
His thighs are alabaster columns,
set upon bases of gold.
He is as tall as a mountain, as strong as cedar.

5:16
His mouth is sweet to the taste,
and he is altogether desirable.
This, O daughters of Jerusalem, is my beloved, my friend.

1 This is an odd question to ask. If Wisdom knows where the seeker is, she would not need the daughters of Jerusalem to conduct a search. Unless the search is less for her and more for you.

The poet may be thinking of God's seeking after Adam in Genesis 3:9, saying, "Where are you?" Could it be that God doesn't know? Is God asking for information or offering the earthling (*adam*, "human," is a play on *adamah*, "earth") an opportunity to step out of hiding and meet God? I suggest that the latter is true. It is the same with this verse: Wisdom knows where you are but needs you to come out of hiding and present yourself to her—to step out from behind the isms and ideology you cling to and be prepared to embrace and be embraced by Wisdom, who has no use for any of them.

2 Throughout the Song of Songs, Wisdom, and Wisdom only, is associated with a garden (4:12) and lilies (2:1). Wisdom is a "private garden" (4:12), meaning that she and she alone controls who has access to her. Yet, here she speaks of "his garden." Is this a reference to a second garden, or is Wisdom now ready to become so intimate with her lover that she no longer distinguishes hers from yours? Given the sexual meaning of the seeker grazing in the garden and gathering lilies, I suggest that the latter is the case.

3 This emerging unity is attested to by Wisdom's affirmation, "I am my beloved's and my beloved is mine." This is similar to, but not identical with, the refrain found in Song 2:16, "My beloved is mine and I am his," where the order is reversed. In the earlier wording you belong to Wisdom; now Wisdom belongs to you. There is a new mutuality emerging with this verse.

☐ Chapter Six

The Daughters of Jerusalem Inquire Further

6:1

Where has your beloved gone, Beautiful One?
Which way has your beloved turned,
that we may seek him with you?[1]

Wisdom Responds

6:2

My beloved has gone down to his garden,[2]
to the beds of spices,
there to graze, and gather lilies.

6:3

I am my beloved's and my beloved is mine;
he grazes among the lilies.[3]

(continued on page 105)

4 Tirzah was the capital of the Northern Kingdom of Israel (1 Kings 14:17), which broke with the Southern Kingdom after the death of King Solomon.

5 Jerusalem was the capital of the Southern Kingdom.

6 With this single verse a dimension of Wisdom is revealed that seems powerfully at odds with the metaphors of gardens and lovemaking: Wisdom as a terrifying force, a violent force, a destructive force. In this, Wisdom reveals her dual nature as both lover and warrior. As warrior she is like the Hindu goddess Kali. Both women are black (Song 1:5), both are decorated with necklaces of war—Kali with the skulls of those she has killed, Wisdom with the shields of those she has vanquished (4:4)—and both ravish you, stripping you of all your defenses. It is terrifying to be naked before Wisdom, to stand without the opinions, labels, and half-truths we use to makes sense out of life. Yet, nothing less will satisfy her.

7 This is the fourth reference to Wisdom's eyes. Twice they are compared to doves (Song 1:15, 4:1), once we are told that a mere glance from her sends you into states of rapture (4:9), and now her gaze shakes you to your core. This reflects a deepening of your relationship with Wisdom. At first she is alluring, then rapturously beautiful, but now she shatters all your illusions, leaving you to face the raw and wild truth of reality.

8 These women represent the theories, ideologies, and isms that claim to be Wisdom but that are at best hallowed opinion. How can you tell the difference? The queens and concubines lead to division, Wisdom to unity; the queens and concubines offer pleasure, and Wisdom offers ecstasy.

The Seeker Speaks

6:4
You are as beautiful as Tirzah, my love,[4]
as breathtaking as Jerusalem,[5]
and yet as terrifying as an army
marching with banners unfurled.[6]

6:5
Lower your gaze, for your eyes make me tremble![7]
Your black hair ripples down your shoulders—
black goats streaming down the slopes of Gilead.

6:6
Your teeth are white and even—
a flock of ewes each with its twin coming up from washing.

6:7
Your cheeks curve like pomegranate halves behind your
veil.

6:8
There are sixty queens and eighty concubines, and virgins
without number.[8]

(continued on page 107)

9 Wisdom is perfect, meaning whole and complete. Wisdom unites the opposites of Tirzah and Jerusalem; all conflict is reconciled in her. This is why she will be called the *Shulamite*, the Woman of Wholeness and Peace (see Song 7:1).

10 Even the queens and concubines are struck by Wisdom's superiority. But they do not know her and can only ask about her from the one who seeks her.

11 In Song 6:2, Wisdom told us that you had gone down to your garden. Here you say that you went down to the walnut grove. In Hebrew the words "garden" (*gan*) and "grove" (*ginah*) share a common Hebrew root, *g-n*, suggesting that the garden and the grove are one and the same. Wisdom throughout the Song is associated with gardens, and the seeker even calls her "woman in the garden" in 8:13.

12 Earlier you rushed the locked gate to the Beloved, and she failed to open to you. You have learned from that and now take your time and wait for your Beloved to bloom.

13 Wisdom takes you into herself with little or no foreplay—much to your surprise! You have reached a level of intimacy that contains moments of near spontaneous union and unexpected ecstasy.

6:9
But one alone is my dove, my perfect one,
precious as an only daughter,[9] the darling of her mother.
The young women call her happy;
and queens and concubines praise her:

> 6:10
> *"Who is this woman striking as dawn,*
> *pure as the moon,*
> *fiery as the sun,*
> *and as terrifying as an army*
> *marching with banners unfurled?"*[10]

The Seeker Speaks

6:11
I descended to the walnut grove,[11]
to view the valley's fruit,
to see whether the vines had budded,
whether the pomegranates were in bloom.[12]

6:12
And before I knew it,
my yearning set me in her most lush chariot![13]

1 The dance here may be the lovemaking of the previous chapter.

2 *Shulamite* is a new name given to Wisdom, and its meaning is unclear. Since *Shulamite* shares the same three-letter Hebrew root— *sh-l-m*— as *shaleim* (complete, whole) and *shalom* (peace), I take *Shulamite* to be "She Who Is Wholeness and Complete Peace."

3 It is the city's guards who demand that Wisdom dance over and over again so they may gaze upon her. The dance is inviting, sensual, and perhaps even sexually stimulating to them, but it is only a pale hint at the ecstasy Wisdom offers you. This verse follows the ecstasy of the seeker thrust into the chariot of Wisdom perhaps to show the contrast between the authentic seeker and mere dilettantes.

4 The Hebrew *machanayim*, "two camps," is first used in Genesis 32:3 by the patriarch Jacob. Taking leave of his father-in-law, Laban, Jacob encounters a camp of angels and calls the place *Machanayim*, a place of encounter between two dimensions: the human and the Divine. The guardians of the status quo see an unbridgeable divide between the human and the Divine, a divide that Wisdom bridges.

The seeker derides the guardians not so much for being captivated by Wisdom's dance but for seeing her in terms of separation rather than unity. This is why he speaks to them of the *Shulamite*, the Woman of Wholeness and Peace. The worldview of the powerful is one of zero-sum competition, where the success of one necessitates the failure of others. The worldview of Wisdom is nonzero, where the success of one is contingent upon the success of all. This is why Wisdom is the *Shulamite*, the Woman Who Is All. It is not enough that you alone become wise; all humanity must do so as well. This is why she sends her maidens out to every city and mountaintop to call all humanity to her (Proverbs 9:3).

☐ Chapter Seven

The Guardians of the City

7:1a
Dance and spin,[1] *Shulamite!*[2]
twirl and twirl again,
that we may gaze upon you.[3]

The Seeker Responds to the Guardians

7:1b
Why should you look upon She Who Is Wholeness and Peace,
as upon a dance between two camps?[4]

(continued on page 111)

5 Heshbon was a northern Israelite city renowned for its fertile soil and luxuriant vineyards.

6 *Bat-rabbim*, literally "Daughter of Many," may be a synonym for Heshbon or a nearby city, or it may be the name of a gate within Heshbon itself.

7 Mount Carmel is a northern mountain in Israel near the Lebanese border and is known for its lush forests. Mount Carmel is often used in the Hebrew Bible to represent fertility: Isaiah 33:9, 35:2; Jeremiah 50:19; Amos 1:2; Nahum 1:4.

The Seeker Speaks to Wisdom

7:2

How graceful are your sandaled feet, noble daughter!
Your thighs round and smooth—the work of a master jeweler.

7:3

Your navel a rounded bowl never lacking nectar.
Your belly a bushel of golden wheat encircled with lilies.

7:4

Your breasts two fawns, twins of a single gazelle.

7:5

Your neck an ivory tower,
your eyes pools in Heshbon[5]
by the gate of *Bat-rabbim*.[6]
Your nose a tower of Lebanon overlooking Damascus.

7:6

Your head rises majestic as Mount Carmel,[7]
and your flowing hair,
a deep and dark purple,
captivates even the mightiest king.

7:7

You are exquisitely beautiful, my love!
More intoxicating than any other pleasure!

(*continued on page 113*)

8 This entire section is a seduction of Wisdom by the seeker. Earlier it was she who seduced you; now it is you who seduces her. The Song is pointing to a growing equality between Wisdom and the seeker of Wisdom.

Apricots are a recurring theme in the Song of Songs. We first encounter them in Song 2:3, where they are a euphemism for her lover's genitals. Two verses later she references them again, asking the seeker to sustain her with apricots for she is "feverish with love" (2:5). In our current verse it is the seeker who speaks of apricots, saying that his Beloved's breath carries their scent. Since this is said in the context of articulating your own desire to "climb" Wisdom and grasp her breasts, the Song may be hinting that you do this after Wisdom has first pleasured you. The final reference to apricots comes from Lady Wisdom, who says that her lover was birthed beneath an apricot tree (see 8:5b).

7:8
You are stately as a date palm,
and your breasts its clustered fruit.

7:9
I said to myself:
"I will climb this palm and grasp its fruit."
Your breasts like clusters of dates on the vine,
the scent of your breath like apricots,[8]

7:10
and your kisses like fine wine
flowing over my mouth
slipping smoothly between my lips.

(continued on page 115)

9 Wisdom affirms her passion for you alone. She can give herself to you fully because, as the rest of the verse says, she knows you have given yourself to her exclusively.

10 Nothing less than Wisdom can satisfy you—not the power and might of Solomon, the authority of the city guards, the adulation or allure of the daughters of Jerusalem, or the pleasures of the sixty queens, eighty concubines, and endless virgins.

11 Again it is important to note that it is Wisdom who initiates intimacy. She must invite you to enter her.

12 Wisdom is here echoing a similar speech of the seeker (Song 6:11). These references to ripening are euphemisms for the ripening of her desire for you and your desire for her.

13 The Hebrew is *dudaim*, "love plants," often translated as "mandrakes." *Dudaim* are mentioned only twice in the Hebrew Bible: here and in Genesis 30:14–16, where they are used as an aphrodisiac. Taken in small quantities *dudaim*, a part of the nightshade family, is a stimulant similar to cocaine. Why would Wisdom mix a love potion? Could it be that there are dimensions of ecstasy that you cannot reach without the assist of a drug? Might this verse hint at the uses of hallucinogens by those who seek Lady Wisdom? Personally I suggest it does, but this is pure speculation.

14 Wisdom's preparations hearken back to Proverbs 9:2, where we are told that Wisdom has prepared a banquet of food and wine for all who seek her. What is this food and wine? The book of Proverbs doesn't say, but here we learn that the wine is a love potion and the food is fruit.

Wisdom Speaks

7:11
I am my beloved's,[9]
and his desire is for me alone.[10]

7:12
Come, my beloved,
let us go out into the fields,
and find lodging in the villages.[11]

7:13
We will rise early and see to the vineyards:
Have the vines budded?
Have the blossoms opened?
Are the pomegranates blooming?[12]
There I will give you my love.

7:14
I have prepared a love potion[13]
whose wild fragrance fills the air,
and on our doors hang the choicest fruits,
ripe as well as unripe.[14]

1 Wisdom has half-brothers whose only desire is to enslave her, and she has no desire to show them any love. What she desires is to kiss you in public, to love you openly, something she could do if you were her brother but cannot do with you as her lover.

In Proverbs 7:13 we are told of a harlot who grabs young men in the street and kisses them in public. Wisdom wants the same freedom as the whore but without the moral approbation that goes with it. She is challenging the moral limits conventional society employs, suggesting, perhaps, that she stands beyond them.

☐ Chapter Eight

Wisdom Speaks

8:1
If you were my brother,
nursed at my mother's breast,
I could kiss you in public,
and none would chastise me.[1]

(*continued on page 119*)

2 This is the second time Lady Wisdom speaks of making love on her mother's bed (see Song 3:4). In that earlier reference Wisdom speaks of her mother as the one who "conceived me." Here she speaks of her mother as the one "who taught me."

What might Wisdom's mother have taught her? Given her association with lovemaking, I suggest she taught Wisdom the arts of sexual arousal and ecstasy necessary to initiate you into the wisdom she wishes to impart, including the making and administering of the *dudaim* potion.

And what is it that Wisdom imparts? Solomon tells us in the Apocryphal book the Wisdom of Solomon:

> A knowledge of basic physics and chemistry, and how things arise, thrive, and pass away. The way seasons and solstices turn and return; the passing of time, and how the stars appear in the night sky. The nature of domesticated animals and the tempers of wild ones. The power of imagination, intuition, and reason. The medicinal use of plants and the healing properties of roots. All this I learned—both the secret and the revealed—for Wisdom the fashioner of all things taught me.
>
> (Wisdom of Solomon 7:17–22)

3 While it is quite easy to read this verse as a euphemism for oral sex, we might take it literally instead: the spice wine is the *dudaim* potion, whose taste is made sweeter with pomegranate juice.

8:2
I would lead you to my mother's house,
the one who taught me,
and upon her bed[2]
I would give you spiced wine
and bid you drink my pomegranate nectar.[3]

(continued on page 121)

4 This passage is similar to that found in Chapter 2:6–7, but with two differences. In this passage the charge to the daughters of Jerusalem is stronger, and all references to gazelles and wild deer are missing. The result is a more intense image of the union of Wisdom and her lover. There is nothing abstract, metaphoric, or even poetic here. It is a flat-out command: do not interrupt us!

Why the more forceful demand to be left alone? I suggest this has to do with the use of the *dudaim*. The drug must be given time to raise your consciousness beyond what sexual pleasure alone can achieve. You must have the time to surrender to its influence so that Wisdom can lift you into the highest dimensions of ecstasy her mother has taught her to achieve and to share. Further still, you may need time to recover from the high Wisdom induces, and this, too, the daughters of Jerusalem might inadvertently interrupt.

5 This question parallels a similar query the daughters make in Song 3:6. In 3:7 the guardians of the city tell the daughters that it is the litter of Solomon they see coming up from the wilderness, carried by armed warriors. In our current verse it isn't Solomon but Wisdom who is coming, and while the king rests on a litter, Wisdom leans on her beloved.

There can be no starker contrast between the worlds of power and worlds of Wisdom, though, as we noted at 3:6, Solomon never actually appears on the litter or even in the Song of Songs. The reason for this is that Solomon is himself a lover of Wisdom, as we learn in Ecclesiastes and the Wisdom of Solomon, two ancient Jewish books of wisdom. What the city guards see is a bed of power they associate with Solomon, but that is their projection and not necessarily Solomon's predilection.

8:3
I yearn for your left hand beneath my head,
your right hand pulling me to you!

8:4
Swear to me, daughters of Jerusalem,
do not disturb our lovemaking until we are through![4]

The Daughters of Jerusalem Inquire

8:5a
Who is this coming up from the wilderness,
leaning upon her beloved?[5]

(continued on page 123)

6 Unlike the guardians of the city who answer the query of the daughters of Jerusalem in Song 3:7, Wisdom herself ignores the daughters and speaks directly to you, on whom she is leaning.

Wisdom's mother conceived her in a bed in a bedchamber. The seeker's mother conceived him outdoors under an apricot tree. Just as Wisdom dreams of making love to you in her mother's bed (3:4) and fantasizes doing the same in 8:2, so she will make love to you in your mother's bed. The mentioning of the mothers is an honoring of the two dimensions Wisdom and her lover unite: the world of the Divine and the world of the human.

7 To seal your heart with Wisdom is to close your heart to ignorance. To mark your arm with Wisdom is to align all your deeds to truth.

8 Wisdom isn't saying that love is stronger than death or that love will conquer death, only that love of Wisdom is as strong—as unstoppable—as death. Once kindled, love of Wisdom marches inevitably to its own end: union with the Beloved.

9 The pursuit of Wisdom must be focused and fierce. Just as nothing can deflect life from culminating in the grave, let nothing distract you from uniting with Wisdom.

10 Even a spark of desire for Wisdom is enough to set you ablaze with the passion you need to embrace the Beloved you seek.

Wisdom Speaks

8:5b
Your mother conceived you in this place
and birthed you beneath this apricot tree,
and it is here that I will awaken you.[6]

8:6
Set me as a seal upon your heart,
as an insignia upon your arm;[7]
for love is as strong as death,[8]
passion as fierce as the grave;[9]
its smallest spark is a flash of fire
igniting an inferno.[10]

(continued on page 125)

11 This verse builds on the previous one. While water can extinguish actual fire, the fire of desire is something else. While storms and floods—tragedy and setback—are a part of life, they cannot diminish your passion for Wisdom.

12 Not everyone who desires Wisdom is willing to go to the trouble of seeking her, wooing her, and embracing her. Like Wisdom's half-brothers, they want to own her, not love her. Like the guardians of the city, they want to control her, not learn from her. They imagine they can buy Wisdom the way one purchases information, but this isn't so. It isn't that Wisdom is more expensive than anything else one can purchase but that the price of Wisdom isn't monetary at all. The price of Wisdom is the surrender of illusion, ideology, power, and control. The very thought of buying Wisdom shows a deep ignorance of the nature of Wisdom. No wonder she scorns those who seek her in this way; they don't know her, let alone love her.

13 Wisdom's brothers, or rather half-brothers, are mentioned in Song 1:6, where Wisdom tells us that they force her to work in their vine-yards, making it impossible for her to tend her own vineyard. They appear at the end of the Song of Songs immediately after Wisdom says she cannot be bought by the wealthy and powerful, and so they speak for those who wish not to own Wisdom but simply to lock her away where she cannot upset the norms of society. As we see in the next verse, however, their efforts also fail; Wisdom is free of all social conventions and invites you to join her in that freedom.

8:7
No storm can extinguish love,
no flood can drown it.[11]
No price can be placed on love,
and any who seek to buy her are fools.[12]

Wisdom's Brothers Speak

8:8
We have a little sister,
whose breasts are but buds.
What shall we do for her when suitors encircle her?

8:9
If she were a wall,
we'd build a silver turret atop her;
if she were a door,
we'd craft a cedar bar across her.[13]

(continued on page 127)

14 Where her half-brothers see her as a child whose breasts are buds (Song 8:8), Wisdom knows herself to be a fully grown woman whose breasts are towers. Wisdom is powerful in her own right and needs no protection, especially not from those who represent the forces that oppose her and seek to imprison her.

15 This is Wisdom as the *Shulamite*: the Woman of Wholeness (*shaleim*) and Peace (*shalom*) (7:1).

16 The Hebrew text here refers to Solomon as *ba'al hamon*, literally "master of multitudes." The Song is once again using the image of King Solomon to represent worldly power: Solomon rules millions, and with all his power and wealth he has secured a vineyard of his own, but he chooses not to cultivate it himself. In this he is like Wisdom's half-brothers, who force her to cultivate their vineyard. Solomon, however, simply hires people to do the work for him, and while he pays well for the services they render, unless one cultivates Wisdom for oneself, there is no union with the Beloved.

This use of Solomon as a stand-in for the wealthy and powerful matches the vision of the city guards who see Solomon as a warrior king (3:7). In the other books attributed to him, Proverbs and Ecclesiastes, and in the collection of his teachings compiled in the Wisdom of Solomon, a very different image of Solomon is offered: Solomon, the philosopher of peace and lover of the *Shulamite*, the Woman of Peace.

17 Despite the efforts of her half-brothers to keep her from tending her own garden, and despite opening her garden to you, the seeker, Wisdom never surrenders her autonomy to anyone. Her garden is hers alone. No matter how intimate you become with Wisdom, still she cannot be possessed, and any attempt to do so only speaks to a lack of understanding.

18 Let the wealthy and powerful keep their wealth and power; Wisdom is something else entirely. The guards' silver comes from tending the gardens of the wealthy and powerful, and they never even dream of having a garden of their own. In this they are even further removed from the garden of Wisdom the Song of Songs celebrates.

Wisdom Responds

8:10
I am a wall,
and my breasts are defensive towers;[14]
but to my beloved's eyes I am a refuge of peace.[15]

8:11
Solomon, mastering multitudes,
also owned a vineyard
but he entrusted it to mercenaries,
paying each a thousand pieces of silver.[16]

8:12
My vineyard is mine alone.[17]
Let Solomon keep his thousands!
Let his guards keep their silver![18]

(continued on page 129)

19 Wisdom calls to everyone, and many strive to hear her, but only the solitary seeker willing to give all for love of wisdom (*philo-sophia*) will succeed.

20 The Song ends almost as it began (2:17), with Wisdom calling to you. While some translators of the Song of Songs hear this final verse as the voice of the seeker adding to the previous verse and his plea that she speak to him, I find this unsatisfying. Wisdom is not playing hard to get. She seeks you no less than you seek her. By choosing to hear Wisdom speak in the final verse of the Song, we come full circle, with Wisdom urging you make love to her and awaken to the ecstasy that is union of lover and Beloved.

The Seeker Speaks

8:13
Woman in the garden,
so many listen for your voice;
let me hear it now.[19]

Wisdom Speaks

8:14
Hurry, my beloved,
be swift as a gazelle or a young stag
upon my mountains of spices![20]

☐ The Path of Ecstasy
How to Use the Song of Songs

In all my years of rabbinic study I cannot remember a single time when the word "ecstasy" was used in the context of Judaism. This shouldn't surprise you; the word is not all that common in any religious setting. "It is hardly recognized that ecstasy is a basic human need, just as much as vitamins and proper nutrition, and that when its positive and life-sustaining forms are repressed it is inevitably sought in violence and cruelty."[1]

The reason ecstasy is so rare is that ecstasy is subversive. The word itself, *ek-stasis*, means to stand apart from the norms to which you are supposed to conform. These norms are the cultural, religious, social, economic, and psychological standards that define your sense of self and determine how you are to act in the world. To stand apart from these norms in moments of ecstasy allows you to question them and perhaps even abandon them. This is not something most civilizations value.

Two thousand years ago Rabbi Akiva complained about drunken revelers singing the Song of Songs in bars as if it were merely a bawdy tale of sexual yearning and consummation. He went so far as to threaten these singers with a loss of entry into heaven for treating the Song in this way. For him the Song of Songs was the "Holy of Holies," the most sacred of the sacred texts of the Hebrew Bible. Clearly he saw something in the Song that the inebriated saloon singers did not.

What he saw in the Song of Songs was a metaphor for God's love of the Jewish people. While his understanding of the Song has been the standard among Jews for two millennia, there is nothing in the Song itself that suggests it is anything more than an erotic love song. Similarly when

Christian commentators claim the Song of Songs as a metaphor of the love of Christ for his church, they, too, are reading into the text. I intend to do no less.

Like Akiva and later Jewish and Christian commentators, I read the Song of Songs through a lens that allows me to see something more than erotic love poetry. And I, like them, read my "something more" into the Song of Songs rather than out of it. The difference between these commentators and myself is that I want to make it clear that I am doing this, and not pretend that my reading is somehow the true reading. On the contrary; it is simply another reading, albeit one that I find of great value.

For me, the Song of Songs is not merely a poem to be read, but a map to be followed. The Song is not simply a description of sexual yearning and lovemaking, but a guide to achieving spiritual awakening through sexual ecstasy. For me, the woman in the Song isn't Israel or the church, but Lady Wisdom, the first of God's creations through whom all life is fashioned. For me, the man in the Song isn't God but you, the seeker of Wisdom. So for me, the Song of Songs needs to be embodied by you if the meaning I bring to it is to be experienced in you.

The erotic nature of the Song of Songs and the explicit lovemaking of which it speaks begs to be lived, but how far you are willing to go in this regard is not for me to say. So let me simply set forth suggestions as to how the Song can be employed in the context of spiritual searching and awakening to Wisdom.

Find a Partner

First, you should read the Song of Songs with a partner. You and your partner must each be capable of fulfilling the role of the *eizer k'negdo*. The word appears in the Bible only once, and that is in Genesis 2:18, when God says it is not good for the earthling to be alone and sets about to make an *eizer k'negdo* to partner with him.

As I mentioned earlier, the Hebrew is far more than the standard English translation "helper" allows. *Eizer* does mean "helper," but in the sense of a rescuer rather than as an assistant: "I am completely destitute, O God. Hurry to my rescue [*eizri*]" (Psalm 70:6). *K'negdo* means "one who is your equal and opposite." An *eizer k'negdo* is someone equal to yourself who has the capacity to stand lovingly against you, call you to be more than you are at the moment, and in this way rescue you from the illusion of separateness and its accompanying alienation suffered by the man (but not the woman) in the Garden of Eden. The *eizer k'negdo* sees your potential for awakening and helps you to realize it.

Reading the Song of Songs with an *eizer k'negdo* is essential to discovering the hidden meaning of the Song and to opening to the wisdom it offers. So please take your time in deciding with whom to share the Song of Songs. This must be a person you trust completely and who trusts you completely as well.

The Setting and Posture

While Lady Wisdom fantasizes about making love with her beloved in bed, most of the actual lovemaking in the Song of Songs takes place outdoors in the fields and citrus groves. Reading the Song outdoors in a beautiful and secluded setting is worth trying, but you can bring the outdoor setting of the Song alive indoors in other ways, especially through the use of fragrances. The Song of Songs speaks over and over again of the intoxicating smell of myrrh, frankincense, cinnamon, and musk. You can create a delightful setting for sharing the Song simply by filling the place in which you are reading it with these fragrances.

Some people imagine that the Song of Songs ought to be shared while sitting together on a bed. You might want to experiment with this, though I would refrain from doing so until you have shared the Song with your *eizer k'negdo* several times in other settings. The Song uses sexual metaphors to lift you to mystical states, and you want to take care not to set yourself up for being distracted from those states by highlighting the sexual elements separated from their capacity to lift you to Wisdom.

You also might imagine that the proper posture for reading the Song of Songs is lying down, but this proves not to be the case. You want to make eye contact with your *eizer k'negdo*, and sitting across from one another on chairs or cushions is conducive to the intimacy you are seeking. The distance between you and your partner will allow you each to focus on the personal and transpersonal aspects of the Song before losing yourself in the interpersonal. From chairs and cushions you may move on to sitting together on a couch or love seat.

There may be moments, however, especially when rubbing one another's feet, hands, and temples with scented oil (more on this in a moment), that a more intimate posture seems natural. The Song of Songs describes this posture this way: place your left hand at the back of your partner's head, and your right hand and arm around your partner's waist, drawing each other close. Be careful to keep enough distance to maintain eye contact and to observe one another's bodies so that when reading the Song's descriptions you can see what you are talking about.

Most readers of the Song make little of this right hand–left hand imagery. Psychologist Robert Ornstein, however, suggests that it may speak to the balancing of the two hemispheres of the brain, or two capacities of mind: intuition (the left hand–right brain) and reason (the right hand–left brain).[2]

Oils, Food, and Drink

In addition to entering into the Song of Songs using the sense of smell, you may want to use the sense of touch and taste as well. Indeed, all five senses are part of the Song, but sight and sound will come naturally from the reading, while smell, touch, and taste need to be cultivated more consciously.

The Song of Songs makes repeated reference to scented oils. Since Lady Wisdom calls herself a rose, I suggest you use rose-scented oil, though you should feel free to experiment with other oils as well. The oils will be massaged into one another's feet, hands, and temples as a way of awakening you from head to toe to the Wisdom that arises between you and within you.

Lady Wisdom speaks of growing faint with passion and uses raisin cakes or apricots to sustain her. You might consider doing the same. There may be moments during your reading when you are losing focus, and it may be wise at such moments to stop, share some cake or fruit, and refocus your energies.

The love Wisdom desires and offers is ecstatic, and she often uses wine as the metaphor for this. Here I agree with Rabbi Akiva that getting drunk while reading the Song or reciting the Song while intoxicated is a mistake. While, unlike Akiva, I don't believe a drunken recital of the Song will cost you your place in heaven, I do believe that it will make it all the more difficult to reach Wisdom. If you choose to drink wine, do so sparingly. If wine isn't to your liking, I suggest pure water, water scented with rose petals, or grape juice.

The Song of Songs speaks of a love potion made of *dudaim* (7:14). *Dudaim* (mandrake) are of the nightshade family of plants and can, when properly used, be a helpful stimulant and aphrodisiac that Lady Wisdom seems to suggest heightens sexual pleasure. The right mixture of this stimulant is lost to us, however, and I do not recommend you experiment with it. I mention the love potion here because it is mentioned in the Song, and not to suggest you concoct one for yourself.

Music

Another way to add to the ambience of your sharing the Song of Songs is to play music in the background. There are several wonderful recordings of verses of the Song, and I encourage you to browse the web for those that speak to you. My only suggestion is that you play the music quietly in the background, an "aural scent" to accompany the olfactory ones provided by incense and spices. Because some of the recordings are English translations of the Hebrew original, playing them too loudly makes your own recitation more difficult and harder to share.

Reading versus Reciting

I want to make a distinction between reading and reciting. When we read, our eyes are fixed on an external text, and our focus is inward. When we recite, the text is internalized, and our focus is outward. You want to recite the Song of Songs rather than read it.

This requires practice. You could, of course, memorize the entire poem, but that is impractical for most people. Instead, glance down at the text, read a line silently to yourself, lift your head, make eye contact with your *eizer k'nego*, and recite the line to your partner.

At first this may feel awkward, but in time you will get comfortable with it. The Song of Songs is both a poem to be recited and a play to be enacted. The scents, food, wine, and oils will help with the latter, but unless you can recite the poem to your partner, the full power of the Song is not realized.

A Fuller Ecstasy

Before we take on this next section, let me remind you once again that "the genitalia are not the only centers of erotic experience; there are circumstances under which the whole organism can become an 'erogenous zone' to such an extent that almost all experience becomes erotic."[3]

The seventh chapter of the Song of Songs is the map for this whole-body arousal. The seeker speaks of Wisdom as a beautiful date palm and vows to climb her. This is where the use of the Song slips into a level of intimacy about which I hesitate to comment and with which you may be uncomfortable. So let us take a half measure and lay out the map, and leave following the map entirely up to you.

Just be clear with yourself and your partner that following this map successfully requires that each of you maintain your role as *eizer k'negdo*: you are going to serve one another the gift of ecstasy for Wisdom's sake and not your own; for the sake of awakening to the Divine within and without, and not for any other purpose whatsoever. If you cannot trust yourself or your partner with this, do not indulge in it.

If you already love your partner, and if you are already sexually intimate with one another, chapter 7 may be of great value to you. If you are not, it can be a terrible stumbling block. Remember it is Wisdom you are seeking to love, and while the love we cultivate is sensual, it needn't be sexual. It is a spiritual love rather than a romantic attraction. Falling romantically in love with your *eizer k'negdo* because of the intimacy evoked by the Song of Songs is a temptation and a trap that you both must do everything to avoid.

That said, here are fragments from the seventh chapter of the Song of Songs with its accompanying practices.

How graceful are your sandaled feet

Begin by massaging your partner's feet with oil.

Your thighs round and smooth

Continue applying the oil to the calves and thighs.

Your navel a rounded bowl never lacking nectar

The navel is a euphemism for one's genitals; here too oils are to be applied.

Your belly a bushel of golden wheat encircled with lilies

Continue the massage up the torso, both front and back.

Your breasts two fawns, twins of a single gazelle

Stimulate your partner's breasts.

Your neck an ivory tower

Massage the neck and shoulders.

your eyes pools in Heshbon by the gate of Bat-rabbim.

Carefully apply oils around the corners of the eyes and temples of the head.

Your nose a tower of Lebanon overlooking Damascus

Gently caress your partner's face.

Your head rises majestic as Mount Carmel

Cradle your partner's head in your arms against your breast.

and your flowing hair, a deep and dark purple

Stroke your partner's hair, and gently massage your partner's head.

I will climb this palm

If you are both ready, this is the moment of sexual union.

Kisses like fine wine flowing over my mouth

The intimacy is absolute.

This map should be followed as a kind of yoga, a spiritual path to awakening to the unity of opposites within and without, that should be done "without conceptualization or seeking a result, such as orgasm.... If the word 'lust' is to designate a vice, it must refer to a mental attitude rather than an organic process, and it seems to me that lust in this sense is precisely a fetishistic fascination with certain 'parts' of the body—the penis, the vagina, the breasts, the buttocks, the feet, the lips, or the nape of the neck."[4] This kind of lust erases the possibility of unity, lifts one body part out of the entire environment of the whole that you are seeking to enter.

In an embrace of this kind [for example, the embrace of Wisdom and seeker presented in the Song of Songs] all considerations of time and place, of what and who, drop away, and that the pair discover themselves as the primordial "love that makes the world go round." There is an extraordinary melting of sensation in which "each is both," and seeing their eyes reflected in each other's they realize that there is one Self looking out through both—and through all eyes everywhen and everywhere. The conceptual boundary between male and female, self and other, dissolves, and—as every spoke leads to the hub—this particular embrace on this particular day discloses itself as going on forever, behind the scenes.[5]

Gazing

The physical contact necessary when following the "instructions" set forth in the seventh chapter of the Song isn't for everyone. An alternative, or if you prefer additional, practice is derived from the Song's passages where the lovers gaze upon and comment on each other's bodies. Assuming you are exploring the Song of Songs with a beloved *eizer k'negdo*, gazing upon one another can itself be a doorway to ecstasy and union.

> Most of our spiritual traditions tell us that, as humans, we are miniature reflections of God and that we have been created in God's image. If this is so, then it would follow that a more direct way to look upon the face of God would be to sit and gaze at an actual person, a real flesh-and-blood human. If he or she will sit and hold your gaze in return, something begins to transpire between the two of you. If you can truly see another and be seen by the other, you begin to see that he or she is an embodiment of the Divine, and you begin to feel that you are as well.[6]

Chapter 4 of the Song of Songs offers us a wonderful example of the seeker gazing at the beauty of Wisdom (4:1–8), and chapter 5 contains an equally fine example of Wisdom gazing upon the seeker (5:10–16). The power of this practice is made explicit in 4:9, "A single glance ... and my heart is raptured."

To engage in gazing, sit across from one another and recite (rather than read) to each other the passages of the Song just mentioned. Experiment with gender here. Regardless of the sex of your *eizer k'nedgo*, read both passages and see how each impacts you. In the end it won't be the gazing at the body of your *eizer k'nedgo* that will trigger the ecstasy, but gazing into her or his eyes.

> It may be that great friends [what we are calling *eizer k'nedgo*] who enter into the practice of gazing at the beloved together will

find that they're drawn to become physical lovers as well ... but it needs to be stressed that the extraordinary merging and profound realization of love that the practice naturally spawn may occur without one body ever physically touching the other. The practice is not one in which, necessarily, physical bodies make love, but one in which souls go out of their minds with the passion of their lovemaking.[7]

After reciting the Song's gazing verses, allow your eyes to gaze into the eyes of the other. Gazing isn't the same as staring. You aren't looking for something, but surrendering to something—the *Shekhinah*, the presence of God manifesting as you both. Keep your eyes soft; rest your gaze on one or another of your *eizer k'negdo*'s eyes, and relax into the gaze as much as you can. Don't resist or engage with any of the feelings that arise; simply accept whatever is happening while you sit still and gaze. Trust that Wisdom knows what she is doing and that all you need to do is remain present to your *eizer k'negdo*.

When you feel it is time to break eye contact and end your mutual gazing, recite the following verse from the Song of Songs as a way of bringing your gazing to a close: *Ani l'dodi v'dodi li*, "I am my beloved's and my beloved is mine" (6:3).

Private Devotion

Not everyone has or desires an *eizer k'negdo* with whom to share the Song of Songs, nor will all readers be attracted to the sensual elements of chapter 7. But this shouldn't rob you of its value as a meditative text. The Song can be read devotionally, an expression of your longing for the Divine Feminine—call her Wisdom, Tao, Kali, God, or what you will. As the Hindu Rig Veda tells us, "Truth is one. Different people call it by different names" (1.64.46).

Read through the Song of Songs and highlight those verses that speak to your longing for Wisdom. Add to these those verses of praise that help you celebrate your beloved. Don't worry about the voice the poem uses. It doesn't matter if it is Wisdom speaking or the seeker. Don't worry about gender at all. Simply highlight the verses that express your love of the Divine and your longing for her.

Then read these aloud. You may still use spices and incense to make your reading a bit more intense, but recite these verses to your beloved however understood. You will find that this method of using the Song of Songs can also bring you a sense of wholeness and peace as you praise and draw near the Woman of Wholeness and Peace.

Notes to Front and Back Matter ☐

Introduction: The Song of Songs as the Holy of Holies

1. *Tosefta, Sanhedrin* 12:10.
2. Babylonian Talmud, *Sanhedrin* 101a.
3. Jewish tradition says that King Solomon wrote the Song of Songs in his youth, Proverbs in middle-age, and Ecclesiastes in old age. Historical data suggests otherwise. All three books were composed centuries after Solomon's death in the tenth century BCE.
4. Babylonian Talmud, *Bava Batra* 14b.
5. *Mishnah Yadayim* 3:5.
6. Elie Assis, *Flashes of Fire: A Literary Analysis of the Song of Songs* (New York: T&T Clark, 2009), 266.
7. Alan Watts, *Nature, Man, and Woman* (New York: Vintage Books, 1970), 11.
8. William Johnston, ed., *The Cloud of Unknowing* (New York: Image Books, 1973), 7.
9. Thomas Moore, *The Soul of Sex: Cultivating Life as an Act of Love* (New York: HarperCollins, 1998), 148.
10. Marvin Meyer, *The Gospel of Thomas* (New York: HarperCollins, 1992), 35.
11. Watts, *Nature, Man, and Woman*, 96.
12. Nosson Scherman, ed., *Tanach*, Stone ed. (Brooklyn: ArtScroll/Mesorah, 1998), 1681.
13. Babylonian Talmud, *Sanhedrin* 37a.
14. Rashi, quoted in Scherman, *Tanach*, 1681.
15. Richard Alfred Norris, *The Song of Songs: Interpreted by Early Christian and Medieval Commentators* (Grand Rapids, MI: Eerdmans, 2003), 1.
16. For example, Joshua 10:13 and 2 Samuel 1:18 both mention the Book of Jasher; Numbers 21:14 speaks of the Book of the Wars of *YHVH*; and 2 Chronicles 9:29, 12:15, and 13:22 mention the Annals of the Prophet Iddo.
17. Gerson Cohen, *Studies in the Variety of Rabbinic Cultures* (New York: Jewish Publication Society, 1991), 11.
18. Ibid., 6.

19. YHVH, derived from the causal form of the Hebrew verb "to be" is the most sacred name of God in Judaism. Often linked to Exodus 3:14 *"Ehyeh asher Ehyeh"* (I will be whatever I will be), YHVH is best understood as the dynamic source of all existence.

20. Cohen, *Studies in the Variety of Rabbinic Cultures*, 12.

21. Saadia Gaon, cited in Marvin H. Pope, *Song of Songs: A New Translation with Introduction and Commentary*, Anchor Bible (Garden City, NY: Doubleday, 1977), 89.

22. Andrew Harvey, *Son of Man: The Mystical Path to Christ* (New York: Jeremy P. Tarcher/Putnam, 1998), 121.

God's Daughter: Wisdom as the Divine Feminine

1. Arthur Waley, *The Way and Its Power: Lao Tzu's Tao Te Ching and Its Place in Chinese Thought* (New York: Grove Press, 1958), 55.

2. Stephen Mitchell, *Tao te Ching: A New English Version* (Radford, VA: Wilder Publications, 2008), 1.

3. Gerhard von Rad, *Old Testament Theology*, vol. 1 (New York: Harper & Row, 1962), 444.

4. Philo, quoted in Gershom Scholem, *On the Mystical Shape of the Godhead: Basic Concepts in the Kabbalah* (New York: Schocken Books, 1991), 144.

5. *Pirke Avot* 3:7.

6. *Midrash Rabbah*, Proverbs 22:29.

7. Scholem, *On the Mystical Shape of the Godhead*, 158.

8. Ibid., 159.

9. Ibid., 160.

10. Ibid., 161–62.

11. Ibid., 164.

12. Ibid., 172.

13. Ibid., 173.

14. Ibid., 174.

15. Ibid., 182.

Back to the Garden: From Eve to the *Shulamite*

1. Gershom Scholem, *On the Mystical Shape of the Godhead: Basic Concepts in the Kabbalah* (New York: Schocken Books, 1991), 183.

2. Babylonian Talmud, *Yevamot* 63b.

3. *Genesis Rabbah* 8:1.

4. J. H. Laenen, *Jewish Mysticism: An Introduction* (Louisville, KY: Westminster John Knox Press, 2001), 79.
5. Augustine, *City of God*, trans. Marcus Dobbs (Peabody, MA: Hendrickson, 2009), 419.
6. Ibid., 428.
7. Alan Watts, *Nature, Man, and Woman* (New York: Vintage Books, 1970), 188.

Through My Flesh I See God: The Song of Songs as Jewish *Maithuna*

1. Phyllis Trible, *God and the Rhetoric of Sexuality* (Minneapolis: Fortress Press, 1978), 165.
2. Thich Nhat Hanh, *The Heart of Understanding: Commentaries on the Prajnaparamita Heart Sutra* (Berkeley, CA: Parallax Press, 2009), 3–4.
3. David Biale, *Eros and the Jews: From Biblical Israel to Contemporary America* (Berkeley: University of California Press, 1997), 31.
4. Zohar 3:296a.
5. Damien Keown, *A Dictionary of Buddhism* (New York: Oxford University Press, 2003), 338.
6. Ananda K. Coomaraswamy, *The Dance of Shiva: Essays on Indian Art & Culture* (Mineola, NY: Dover, 2011), 65.
7. Jay Michaelson, *God in Your Body: Kabbalah, Mindfulness and Embodied Spiritual Practice* (Woodstock, VT: Jewish Lights, 2007), 27.
8. Biale, *Eros and the Jews*, 144.
9. Michaelson, *God in Your Body*, 63.
10. *Genesis Rabbah* 8.
11. Andrew Harvey, *Son of Man: The Mystical Path to Christ* (New York: Jeremy P. Tarcher/Putnam, 1998), 121
12. David Gordon White, *The Alchemical Body: Siddha Traditions in Medieval India* (Chicago: University of Chicago Press, 1996), 4–5.
13. Norman O. Brown, *Life against Death: The Psychoanalytical Meaning of History* (Middletown, CT: Wesleyan University Press, 1959), 32.
14. Ibid., 48.
15. Seymour J. Cohen, *Holy Letter: A Study in Jewish Sexual Morality* (New York: Ktav, 1976), 30.
16. Meir ibn Gabbai, quoted in Sherwin Byron and Seymour Cohen, *How to Be a Jew: Ethical Teachings of Judaism* (Northvale, NJ: Jason Aronson, 1992), 154.
17. Cohen, *Holy Letter*, 34.

18. Byron L. Sherwin, "The Human Body: A House of God," in Seymour J. Cohen et al., eds., *Threescore and Ten: Essays in Honor of Rabbi Seymour J. Cohen* (New York: Ktav, 1991), 101.

19. Cohen, *Holy Letter*, 28.

20. Ibid., 31.

21. Lalita Sinah, *Unveiling the Garden of Love: Mystical Symbolism in Layla Majnun & Gita Govinda* (Bloomington, IN: World Wisdom, 2008), 4.

22. Ibid.

23. Ibid., 45.

24. Graham M. Schweig, *Dance of Divine Love* (Princeton, NJ: Princeton University Press, 2005), 8.

25. David L. Haberman, *The Bhaktirasamrtasindhu of Rupa Gosvamin* (New Delhi: Motilal Banarsidass, 2003), 65.

26. Barbara Stoler Miller, *Love Song of the Dark Lord: Jayadeva's Gitagovinda* (New York: Columbia University Press, 1977), 99.

27. Sinah, *Unveiling the Garden of Love*, 45–46.

28. Ibid., 46.

29. Schweig, *Dance of Divine Love*, 183.

30. Trible, *God and the Rhetoric of Sexuality*, 144.

31. Ibid., 161.

32. Ibid., 153.

The Path of Ecstasy: How to Use the Song of Songs

1. Alan Watts, *Erotic Spirituality: The Vision of Konarak* (New York: Collier Books, 1974), 72.

2. Robert Ornstein, *The Psychology of Consciousness* (New York: Viking, 1972), 56–72.

3. Watts, *Erotic Spirituality*, 80.

4. Ibid., 82.

5. Ibid., 89.

6. Will Johnson, *The Spiritual Practices of Rumi: Radical Techniques for Beholding the Divine* (Rochester, VT: Inner Traditions, 2007), 6.

7. Ibid., 41.

Bibliography □

Alter, Robert. *The Art of Biblical Poetry*. Philadelphia: Basic Books, 2011.

Assis, Elie. *Flashes of Fire: A Literary Analysis of the Song of Songs*. New York: T&T Clark International, 2009.

Astell, Ann W. *The Song of Songs in the Middle Ages*. Ithaca, NY: Cornell University Press, 1990.

Augustine. *City of God*. Translated by Marcus Dobbs. Peabody, MA: Hendrickson, 2009.

Barnstone, Willis. *The Gnostic Bible*. Boston: Shambhala, 2003.

———. *The Song of Songs: Shir Hashirim*. Los Angeles: Green Integer, 2002.

Baskin, Judith. *Midrashic Women: Formations of the Feminine in Rabbinic Literature*. Hanover, NH: University Press of New England, 2002.

Bataille, George. *Eroticism: Death and Sensuality*. Translated by Mary Dalwood. San Francisco: City Lights Books, 1986.

Belser, Julia Watts. "Speaking of Goddess: Finding the Sacred Feminine in the Song of Songs." *Zeek*, Spring 2009, 43.

Bergant, Dianne. *Israel's Wisdom Literature: A Liberation–Critical Reading*. Minneapolis: Fortress Press, 1997.

Bernard of Clairvaux. *On the Song of Songs*. Kalamazoo: Cistercian Publications, 1971.

Biale, David. *Eros and the Jews: From Biblical Israel to Contemporary America*. Berkeley: University of California Press, 1997.

Bloch, Ariel, and Chana Bloch. *The Song of Songs: The World's First Great Love Poem*. New York: Modern Library, 2006.

Bose, Mandakranta. *Faces of the Feminine in Ancient, Medieval, and Modern India*. Delhi: Oxford University Press, 2000.

Bourgeault, Cynthia. *The Meaning of Mary Magdalene*. Boston: Shambhala, 2010.

———. *The Wisdom Jesus: Transforming Heart and Mind; a New Perspective on Christ and His Message*. Boston: New Seeds Books, 2008.

———. *The Wisdom Way of Knowing*. San Francisco: Jossey-Bass, 2003.

Boyarin, Daniel. "The Song of Songs, Lock or Key: The Holy Song as a Mashal." In *Intertextuality and the Reading of Midrash*, 105–16. Bloomington: Indiana University Press, 1994.

Brenner, Athalya, and Carole R. Fontaine. *The Song of Songs*. Sheffield, UK: Sheffield Academic Press, 2000.

Brown, Norman O. *Life against Death: The Psychoanalytical Meaning of History*. Middletown, CT: Wesleyan University Press, 1959.

———. *Love's Body*. Los Angeles: University of California Press, 1990.

Bruner, Jerome. *On Knowing: Essays for the Left Hand*. New York: Atheneum, 1971.

Byron, Sherwin, and Seymour Cohen. *How to Be a Jew: Ethical Teachings of Judaism*. Northvale, NJ: Jason Aronson, 1992.

Campbell, Joseph. *Goddesses: Mysteries of the Feminine Divine*. New York: New World Library, 2013.

Cohen, Gerson. *Studies in the Variety of Rabbinic Cultures*. New York: Jewish Publication Society, 1991.

Cohen, Seymour J. *Holy Letter: A Study in Jewish Sexual Morality*. New York: Ktav, 1976.

Cohen, Seymour J., Abraham J. Karp, Louis Jacobs, and Haim Z. Dimitrovsky, eds. *Threescore and Ten: Essays in Honor of Rabbi Seymour J. Cohen*. New York: Ktav, 1991.

Coomaraswamy, Ananda K. *The Dance of Shiva: Essays on Indian Art & Culture*. Mineola, NY: Dover, 2011.

Copeland, Shawn. *The Subversive Power of Love*. Mahwah, NJ: Paulist Press, 2009.

Crenshaw, James. *Studies in Ancient Israelite Wisdom*. New York: Ktav, 1976.

Dasgupta, Shashibhushan. *An Introduction to Tantric Buddhism*. Boston: Shambhala, 1976.

Davis, Ellen. *Proverbs, Ecclesiastes, and the Song of Songs*. Louisville, KY: John Knox Press, 2000.

D'Este, Sorita. *The Cosmic Shekinah*. London: Avalonia, 2010.

Doniger, Wendy. *The Hindus: An Alternative History*. New York: Penguin Press, 2009.

Edwards, Lawrence. *Awakening Kundalini: The Path to Radical Freedom*. Boulder, CO: Sounds True, 2013.

Eliade, Mircea. *The Sacred and the Profane*. Orlando, FL: Harcourt, 1987.

Feuersteing, Georg. *Tantra: Path of Ecstasy*. Boston: Shambhala, 1998.

Freehof, Solomon B. "The Song of Songs: A General Suggestion." *Jewish Quarterly Review*, n.s., 39, no. 4 (April 1949): 397–402.

Gimbutas, Marija. *The Language of the Goddess*. London: Thames and Hudson, 2001.

Ginsberg, H. L. *The Five Meggilloth and Jonah*. New York: Jewish Publication Society, 2008.

Gollancz, Hermann. *The Targum to the Song of Songs*. London: Luzac, 1908.

Guidi, Angela. *Amour et Sagesse: Les Dialogues d'amour de Juda Abravanel dans la tradition salomonienne*. Boston: Brill, 2011.

Haberman, David L. *The Bhaktirasamrtasindhu of Rupa Gosvamin*. New Delhi: Motilal Banarsidass, 2003.

Hammer, Jill. *The Hebrew Priestess*. Teaneck, NJ: Ben Yehuda Press, 2014.

Harding, Elizabeth. *Kali: The Black Goddess of Dakshineswar*. York Beach, MN: Nicolas-Hays, 1993.

Harvey, Andrew. *Son of Man: The Mystical Path to Christ*. New York: Jeremy P. Tarcher/Putnam, 1998.

Hawley, John. *The Divine Consort*. Boston: Beacon Press, 1982.

Hornsby, Teresa J. *Sex Texts from the Bible: Selections Annotated and Explained*. Woodstock, VT: SkyLight Paths, 2007.

Idel, Moshe. *Kabbalah and Eros*. New Haven, CT: Yale University Press, 2005.

———. "Sexual Metaphors and Praxis in the Kabbalah." In *The Jewish Family: Metaphor and Memory*, edited by David Kraemer, 197–224. New York: Oxford University Press, 1989.

Jastrow, Morris. *The Song of Songs*. Philadelphia: J.B. Lippincott, 1921.

Jayadeva. *Gita Govinda*. Translated by Puran Singh and Paul Smith. Victoria, Australia: New Humanity Books, 2013.

John of the Cross. *A Spiritual Canticle of the Soul and the Bridegroom Christ*. Translated by David Lewis. Veritatis Splendor Publications, 2013.

Johnson, Will. *The Spiritual Practices of Rumi: Radical Techniques for Beholding the Divine*. Rochester, VT: Inner Traditions, 2007.

Johnston, William, ed. *The Cloud of Unknowing*. New York: Image Books, 1973.

Keown, Damien. *A Dictionary of Buddhism*. New York: Oxford University Press, 2003.

Kinbar, Carl. *Song of Songs Rabbah: Texts and Study Guide*. Austin, TX: Mechon Messiah, 2012.

The Koren Megillat Shir Hashirim: A Hebrew/English Illustrated Song of Songs. Illustrated by Ze'ev Raban. Jerusalem: Koren Publishers, 2008.

Kraemer, David. *The Jewish Family: Metaphor and Memory*. New York: Oxford University Press, 1989.

Kravitz, Leonar, and Kerry Olitzky. *Shir HaShirim: A Modern Commentary on the Song of Songs*. New York: URJ Press, 2004.

Krishna, Gopi. *Kundalini: The Evolutionary Energy in Man*. Boston: Shambhala, 1997.

Kvam, Krisen. *Eve & Adam: Jewish, Christian, and Muslim Readings on Genesis and Gender*. Bloomington: Indiana University Press, 1999.

Lanzetta, Beverly. *Radical Wisdom: Feminine Mystical Theology*. Minneapolis: Augsburg Fortress, 2005.

Laenen, J. H. *Jewish Mysticism: An Introduction*. Louisville, KY: Westminster John Knox Press, 2001.

Lawson, R. P. *Origen: The Song of Songs, Commentary and Homilies*. London: Longmans, Green, 1957.

Le Guin, Ursula. *Lao Tzu: Tao Te Ching: A Book about the Way and the Power of the Way*. Boston: Shambhala, 1997.

Lila, Sri Devi. *Shakti: Realm of the Divine Mother*. Rochester, VT: Inner Traditions, 2006.

Littledale, Richard F. *A Commentary on the Song of Songs from Ancient and Mediaeval Sources*. London: Joseph Masters, 1869.

Loewe, Raphael. "Apologetic Motifs in the Targum to the Song of Songs." In *Biblical Motifs: Origins and Transformations*, edited by Alexander Altmann, 159–96. Cambridge, MA: Harvard University Press, 1966.

Mair, Victor. *Tao Te Ching*. New York: Bantam Doubleday Dell, 1990.

Maller, Alen S. *God, Sex, and the Kabbalah*. Ridgefield, CT: Ridgefield, 1983.

Matter, Ann E. *The Voice of My Beloved: Song of Songs in Western Medieval Christianity*. Philadelphia: University of Pennsylvania Press, 1990.

Matthews, Caitlin. *Sophia: Goddess of Wisdom and Bride of God*. Wheaton, IL: Quest Books, 2001.

Mead, G. R. S. *The Hymn of Jesus*. Whitefish, MT: Kessinger, 2010.

Menn, E. M. "Targum of the Song of Songs and the Dynamics of Historical Allegory." In *The Interpretation of Scripture in Early Judaism and Christianity: Studies in Language and Tradition*, 423–45. Journal for the Study of the Pseudepigrapha Supplement Series. Sheffield, UK: Sheffield Academic Press, 2000.

Meyer, Marvin. *The Gospel of Thomas*. New York: HarperCollins, 1992.

Michaelson, Jay. *God in Your Body: Kabbalah, Mindfulness and Embodied Spiritual Practice*. Woodstock, VT: Jewish Lights, 2007.

Miller, Barbara Stoler. *Love Song of the Dark Lord: Jayadeva's Gitagovinda*. New York: Columbia University Press, 1977.

Mitchell, Stephen. *Tao Te Ching: A New English Version*. Radford, VA: Wilder, 2008.

Mookerjee, Ajit. *Kundalini: The Arousal of the Inner Energy*. London: Thames & Hudson, 2003.

———. *Kali: The Feminine Force*. Rochester, VT: Destiny Books, 1988.

———. *Kundalini: The Tantric Way: Art, Science, Ritual*. Rochester, VT: Destiny Books, 1981.

Moore, Thomas. *The Soul of Sex: Cultivating Life as an Act of Love*. New York: HarperCollins, 1998.

Muffs, Yochanan. *Love and Joy: Law, Language and Religion in Ancient Israel*. New York: Jewish Theological Seminary, 1992.

Murphy, Roland E. *The Tree of Life: An Exploration of Biblical Wisdom Literature*. Grand Rapids, MI: Eerdmans, 1990.

Netanyahu, Benzion. *Don Isaac Abravanel: Statesman and Philosopher*. New York: Jewish Publication Society, 1972.

Neumann, Erich. *The Great Mother*. Princeton, NJ: University of Princeton Press, 1972.

Neusner, Jacob. *Song of Songs Rabbah: A Theological Commentary to the Midrash*. Lanham, MD: University of America, 2001.

Nhat Hanh, Thich. *The Heart of Understanding: Commentaries on the Prajnaparamita Heart Sutra*. Berkeley, CA: Parallax Press, 2009.

Nizami. *The Story of Layla and Majnun*. London: John Blake, 1997.

Norris, Richard Alfred. *The Song of Songs: Interpreted by Early Christian and Medieval Commentators*. Grand Rapids, MI: Eerdmans, 2003.

Novick, Leah. *On the Wings of Shekhinah: Rediscovering Judaism's Divine Feminine*. Wheaton, IL: Quest Books, 2008.

Ornstein, Robert. *The Psychology of Consciousness*. New York: Viking, 1972.

Ostow, Mortimer. *Ultimate Intimacy: The Psychodynamics of Jewish Mysticism*. London: Karnac Books, 1995.

Pardes, Ilana. *Countertraditions in the Bible: A Feminist Approach*. Cambridge, MA: Harvard University Press, 1993.

Patai, Raphael. *The Hebrew Goddess*. Detroit: Wayne State University Press, 1990.

Paulson, Genevieve. *Kundalini and the Chakras: Evolution in this Lifetime*. Woodbury, MN: Llewellyn, 2002.

Pennington, Basil. *The Song of Songs: A Spiritual Commentary*. Woodstock, VT: SkyLight Paths, 2004.

Perdue, Leo G. *Wisdom and Creation: The Theology of Wisdom Literature*. Nashville, TN: Abingdon, 1994.

Pope, Marvin H. *Song of Songs: A New Translation with Introduction and Commentary*. Anchor Bible. Garden City, NY: Doubleday, 1977.

Powers, John. *Introduction to Tibetan Buddhism*. Boulder, CO: Snow Lion, 2007.

Preece, Rob. *The Psychology of Buddhist Tantra*. Ithaca, NY: Snow Lion, 2006.

Rankin, Oliver. *Israel's Wisdom Literature*. Edinburgh: T&T Clark, 1964.

Rowley, H. H. "The Meaning of 'The Shulamite.'" *American Journal of Semitic Languages and Literatures* 56, no. 1 (January 1939): 84–91.

Scherman, Nosson, ed. *Tanach*. Stone ed. Brooklyn, NY: ArtScroll/Mesorah, 1998.

Scholem, Gershom. *Jewish Gnosticism, Merkabah Mysticism, and Talmudic Tradition*. New York: Jewish Theological Seminary Press, 2012.

———. *On the Kabbalah and Its Symbolism*. New York: Schocken Books, 1965.

———. *On the Mystical Shape of the Godhead: Basic Concepts in the Kabbalah*. New York: Schocken Books, 1991.

Schweig, Graham M. *Dance of Divine Love*. Princeton, NJ: Princeton University Press, 2005.

Shapiro, Rami. *The Divine Feminine in Biblical Wisdom Literature: Selections Annotated & Explained*. Woodstock, VT: SkyLight Paths, 2005.

———. *Ecclesiastes: Annotated & Explained*. Woodstock, VT: SkyLight Paths, 2010.

———. *Ethics of the Sages: Pirke Avot—Annotated & Explained*. Woodstock, VT: SkyLight Paths, 2006.

———. *Perennial Wisdom for the Spiritually Independent: Sacred Teachings— Annotated & Explained*. Woodstock, VT: SkyLight Paths, 2013.

———. *Proverbs: Annotated & Explained*. Woodstock, VT: SkyLight Paths, 2011.

Simon, Maurice. "Midrash Rabbah: Song of Songs." In *Midrash Rabbah: Translated into English with Notes, Glossary and Indices*. Edited by Harry Freedman and Maurice Simon. London: Soncino Press, 1983.

Sinah, Lalita. *Unveiling the Garden of Love: Mystical Symbolism in Layla Majnun & Gita Govinda*. Bloomington, IN: World Wisdom, 2008.

Tigunait, Pandit Rajmani. *Tantra Unveiled*. Honesdale, PA: Himalayan Institute Press, 1999.

Treat, Jay C. "The Aramaic Targum to Song of Songs." Website of Jay C. Treat, PhD. http://ccat.sas.upenn.edu/~jtreat/song/targum/.

Trible, Phyllis. *God and the Rhetoric of Sexuality*. Philadelphia: Fortress Press, 1978.

———. *Texts of Terror: Literary-Feminist Readings of Biblical Narratives*. Philadelphia: Fortress Press, 1984.

von Rad, Gerhard. *Old Testament Theology*. New York: Harper & Row, 1962.

Waley, Arthur. *The Way and Its Power: Lao Tzu's Tao Te Ching and Its Place in Chinese Thought*. New York: Grove Press, 1958.

Wallis, Christopher. *Tantra Illuminated: The Philosophy, History, and Practice of a Timeless Tradition*. Petaluma, CA: Mattamayura Press, 2013.

Watts, Alan. *Erotic Spirituality: The Vision of Konarak*. New York: Collier Books, 1974.

———. *Nature, Man, and Woman*. New York: Vintage Books, 1970.

White, David Gordon. *The Alchemical Body: Siddha Traditions in Medieval India*. Chicago: University of Chicago Press, 1996.

Woodroffe, Sir John. *Shakti and Shakta*. New York: Dover Publications, 1978.

———. *The World as Power*. Manipal, India: Ganesh & Company, 1974.

Yeshe, Lama Thubten. *The Bliss of Inner Fire: Heart Practices of the Six Yogas of Naropa*. Somerville, MA: Wisdom Publications, 1998.

———. *Introduction to Tantra: The Transformation of Desire*. Somerville, MA: Wisdom Publications, 2001.

Zehr, Leslie. *The Alchemy of Dance*. Bloomington, IN: IUniverse, 2008.

Zlotowitz, Meir. *Shir Hashirim/Song of Songs: An Allegorical Translation*. Brooklyn: ArtScroll, 2000.

Inspiration

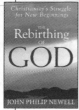

The Rebirthing of God
Christianity's Struggle for New Beginnings
By John Philip Newell
Drawing on modern prophets from East and West, and using the holy island of Iona as an icon of new beginnings, Celtic poet, peacemaker and scholar John Philip Newell dares us to imagine a new birth from deep within Christianity, a fresh stirring of the Spirit.
6 x 9, 160 pp, HC, 978-1-59473-542-4 **$19.99**

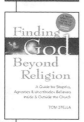

Finding God Beyond Religion: A Guide for Skeptics, Agnostics & Unorthodox Believers Inside & Outside the Church
By Tom Stella; Foreword by The Rev. Canon Marianne Wells Borg
Reinterprets traditional religious teachings central to the Christian faith for people who have outgrown the beliefs and devotional practices that once made sense to them.
6 x 9, 160 pp, Quality PB, 978-1-59473-485-4 **$16.99**

Fully Awake and Truly Alive: Spiritual Practices to Nurture Your Soul
By Rev. Jane E. Vennard; Foreword by Rami Shapiro
Illustrates the joys and frustrations of spiritual practice, offers insights from various religious traditions and provides exercises and meditations to help us become more fully alive.
6 x 9, 208 pp, Quality PB, 978-1-59473-473-1 **$16.99**

Journeys of Simplicity: Traveling Light with Thomas Merton, Bashō, Edward Abbey, Annie Dillard & Others   By Philip Harnden
Invites you to consider a more graceful way of traveling through life. PB includes journal pages to help you get started on your own spiritual journey.
5½ x 7¼, 144 pp, Quality PB, 978-1-59473-181-5 **$12.99**
5½ x 7¼, 128 pp, HC, 978-1-893361-76-8 **$16.95**

Perennial Wisdom for the Spiritually Independent
Sacred Teachings—Annotated & Explained
Annotation by Rami Shapiro; Foreword by Richard Rohr
Weaves sacred texts and teachings from the world's major religions into a coherent exploration of the five core questions at the heart of every religion's search.
5½ x 8½, 336 pp, Quality PB Original, 978-1-59473-515-8 **$16.99**

Saving Civility: 52 Ways to Tame Rude, Crude & Attitude for a Polite Planet
By Sara Hacala
Provides fifty-two practical ways you can reverse the course of incivility and make the world a more enriching, pleasant place to live.
6 x 9, 240 pp, Quality PB, 978-1-59473-314-7 **$16.99**

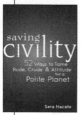

Spiritually Healthy Divorce: Navigating Disruption with Insight & Hope
By Carolyne Call
A spiritual map to help you move through the twists and turns of divorce.
6 x 9, 224 pp, Quality PB, 978-1-59473-288-1 **$16.99**

Or phone, fax, mail or email to: SKYLIGHT PATHS Publishing
Sunset Farm Offices, Route 4 • P.O. Box 237 • Woodstock, Vermont 05091
Tel: (802) 457-4000 • Fax: (802) 457-4004 • www.skylightpaths.com
Credit card orders: (800) 962-4544 (8:30AM–5:30PM EST Monday–Friday)
Generous discounts on quantity orders. SATISFACTION GUARANTEED. Prices subject to change.

Bible Study / Midrash

Passing Life's Tests: Spiritual Reflections on the Trial of Abraham, the Binding of Isaac *By Rabbi Bradley Shavit Artson, DHL*
Invites us to use this powerful tale as a tool for our own soul wrestling, to confront our existential sacrifices and enable us to face—and surmount—life's tests.
6 x 9, 176 pp, Quality PB, 978-1-58023-631-7 **$18.99**

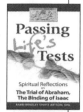

Speaking Torah: Spiritual Teachings from around the Maggid's Table—in Two Volumes *By Arthur Green, with Ebn Leader, Ariel Evan Mayse and Or N. Rose*
The most powerful Hasidic teachings made accessible—from some of the world's preeminent authorities on Jewish thought and spirituality.
Volume 1—6 x 9, 512 pp, Hardcover, 978-1-58023-668-3 **$34.99**
Volume 2—6 x 9, 448 pp, Hardcover, 978-1-58023-694-2 **$34.99**

A Partner in Holiness: Deepening Mindfulness, Practicing Compassion and Enriching Our Lives through the Wisdom of R. Levi Yitzhak of Berdichev's *Kedushat Levi*
By Rabbi Jonathan P. Slater, DMin; Foreword by Arthur Green; Preface by Rabby Nancy Flam
Contemporary mindfulness and classical Hasidic spirituality are brought together to inspire a satisfying spiritual life of practice.
Volume 1— 6 x 9, 336 pp, HC, 978-1-58023-794-9 **$35.00**
Volume 2— 6 x 9, 288 pp, HC, 978-1-58023-795-6 **$35.00**

The Genesis of Leadership: What the Bible Teaches Us about Vision, Values and Leading Change *By Rabbi Nathan Laufer; Foreword by Senator Joseph I. Lieberman*
6 x 9, 288 pp, Quality PB, 978-1-58023-352-1 **$18.99**

Hineini in Our Lives: Learning How to Respond to Others through 14 Biblical Texts and Personal Stories *By Rabbi Norman J. Cohen, PhD*
6 x 9, 240 pp, Quality PB, 978-1-58023-274-6 **$18.99**

Masking and Unmasking Ourselves: Interpreting Biblical Texts on Clothing & Identity *By Dr. Norman J. Cohen*
6 x 9, 224 pp, HC, 978-1-58023-461-0 **$24.99**

The Messiah and the Jews: Three Thousand Years of Tradition, Belief and Hope
By Rabbi Elaine Rose Glickman; Foreword by Rabbi Neil Gillman, PhD;
Preface by Rabbi Judith Z Abrams, PhD 6 x 9, 192 pp, Quality PB, 978-1-58023-690-4 **$16.99**

The Modern Men's Torah Commentary: New Insights from Jewish Men on the 54 Weekly Torah Portions *Edited by Rabbi Jeffrey K. Salkin*
6 x 9, 368 pp, HC, 978-1-58023-395-8 **$24.99**

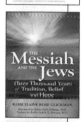

Moses and the Journey to Leadership: Timeless Lessons of Effective Management from the Bible and Today's Leaders *By Rabbi Norman J. Cohen, PhD*
6 x 9, 240 pp, Quality PB, 978-1-58023-351-4 **$18.99**; HC, 978-1-58023-227-2 **$21.99**

The Other Talmud—The Yerushalmi: Unlocking the Secrets of The Talmud of Israel for Judaism Today *By Rabbi Judith Z. Abrams, PhD*
6 x 9, 256 pp, HC, 978-1-58023-463-4 **$24.99**

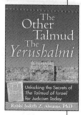

Sage Tales: Wisdom and Wonder from the Rabbis of the Talmud
By Rabbi Burton L. Visotzky
6 x 9, 256 pp, Quality PB, 978-1-58023-791-8 **$19.99**; HC, 978-1-58023-456-6 **$24.99**

The Torah Revolution: Fourteen Truths That Changed the World
By Rabbi Reuven Hammer, PhD 6 x 9, 240 pp, HC, 978-1-58023-457-3 **$24.99**

The Wisdom of Judaism: An Introduction to the Values of the Talmud
By Rabbi Dov Peretz Elkins 6 x 9, 192 pp, Quality PB, 978-1-58023-327-9 **$16.99**

Or phone, fax, mail or email to: **JEWISH LIGHTS** Publishing
Sunset Farm Offices, Route 4 • P.O. Box 237 • Woodstock, Vermont 05091
Tel: (802) 457-4000 • Fax: (802) 457-4004 • www.jewishlights.com
Credit card orders: **(800) 962-4544** (8:30AM–5:30PM EST Monday–Friday)
Generous discounts on quantity orders. SATISFACTION GUARANTEED. Prices subject to change.

Spiritual Poetry—The Mystic Poets

Experience these mystic poets as you never have before. Each beautiful, compact book includes a brief introduction to the poet's time and place, a summary of the major themes of the poet's mysticism and religious tradition, essential selections from the poet's most important works, and an appreciative preface by a contemporary spiritual writer.

Hafiz
The Mystic Poets
Translated and with Notes by Gertrude Bell
Preface by Ibrahim Gamard
Hafiz is known throughout the world as Persia's greatest poet, with sales of his poems in Iran today only surpassed by those of the Qur'an itself. His probing and joyful verse speaks to people from all backgrounds who long to taste and feel divine love and experience harmony with all living things.
5 x 7¼, 144 pp, HC, 978-1-59473-009-2 **$16.99**

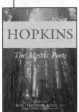

Hopkins
The Mystic Poets
Preface by Rev. Thomas Ryan, CSP
Gerard Manley Hopkins, Christian mystical poet, is beloved for his use of fresh language and startling metaphors to describe the world around him. Although his verse is lovely, beneath the surface lies a searching soul, wrestling with and yearning for God.
5 x 7¼, 112 pp, HC, 978-1-59473-010-8 **$16.99**

Tagore
The Mystic Poets
Preface by Swami Adiswarananda
Rabindranath Tagore is often considered the Shakespeare of modern India. A great mystic, Tagore was the teacher of W. B. Yeats and Robert Frost, the close friend of Albert Einstein and Mahatma Gandhi, and the winner of the Nobel Prize for Literature. This beautiful sampling of Tagore's two most important works, *The Gardener* and *Gitanjali*, offers a glimpse into his spiritual vision that has inspired people around the world.
5 x 7¼, 144 pp, HC, 978-1-59473-008-5 **$16.99**

Whitman
The Mystic Poets
Preface by Gary David Comstock
Walt Whitman was the most innovative and influential poet of the nineteenth century. This beautiful sampling of Whitman's most important poetry from *Leaves of Grass*, and selections from his prose writings, offers a glimpse into the spiritual side of his most radical themes—love for country, love for others and love of self.
5 x 7¼, 192 pp, HC, 978-1-59473-041-2 **$16.99**

Sacred Texts

JUDAISM

Embracing the Divine Feminine: Finding God through the Ecstasy of Physical Love—The Song of Songs Annotated & Explained
By Rabbi Rami Shapiro; Foreword by Rev. Cynthia Bourgeault, PhD
Restores the Song of Songs' eroticism and interprets it as a celebration of the love between the Divine Feminine and the contemporary spiritual seeker.
5½ x 8½, 176 pp, Quality PB, 978-1-59473-575-2 **$16.99**

The Book of Job: Annotated & Explained
Translation and Annotation by Donald Kraus; Foreword by Dr. Marc Brettler
Clarifies for today's readers what Job is, how to overcome difficulties in the text, and what it may mean for us. 5½ x 8½, 256 pp, Quality PB, 978-1-59473-389-5 **$16.99**

The Divine Feminine in Biblical Wisdom Literature
Selections Annotated & Explained
Translation & Annotation by Rabbi Rami Shapiro; Foreword by Rev. Cynthia Bourgeault, PhD
Uses the Hebrew Bible and Wisdom literature to explain Sophia's way of wisdom and illustrate Her creative energy. 5½ x 8½, 240 pp, Quality PB, 978-1-59473-109-9 **$16.99**

Ecclesiastes: Annotated & Explained
Translation & Annotation by Rabbi Rami Shapiro; Foreword by Rev. Barbara Cawthorne Crafton
A timeless teaching on living well amid uncertainty and insecurity.
5½ x 8½, 160 pp, Quality PB, 978-1-59473-287-4 **$16.99**

Ethics of the Sages: Pirke Avot—Annotated & Explained
Translation & Annotation by Rabbi Rami Shapiro
Clarifies the ethical teachings of the early Rabbis. 5½ x 8½, 192 pp, Quality PB, 978-1-59473-207-2 **$16.99**

Hasidic Tales: Annotated & Explained
Translation & Annotation by Rabbi Rami Shapiro; Foreword by Andrew Harvey
Introduces the legendary tales of the impassioned Hasidic rabbis, presenting them as stories rather than as parables. 5½ x 8½, 240 pp, Quality PB, 978-1-893361-86-7 **$18.99**

The Hebrew Prophets: Selections Annotated & Explained
Translation & Annotation by Rabbi Rami Shapiro; Foreword by Rabbi Zalman M. Schachter-Shalomi
5½ x 8½, 224 pp, Quality PB, 978-1-59473-037-5 **$16.99**

Maimonides—Essential Teachings on Jewish Faith & Ethics
The Book of Knowledge & the Thirteen Principles of Faith—Annotated & Explained
Translation and Annotation by Rabbi Marc D. Angel, PhD
Opens up for us Maimonides's views on the nature of God, providence, prophecy, free will, human nature, repentance and more. 5½ x 8½, 224 pp, Quality PB, 978-1-59473-311-6 **$18.99**

Proverbs: Annotated & Explained
Translation and Annotation by Rabbi Rami Shapiro
Demonstrates how these complex poetic forms are actually straightforward instructions to live simply, without rationalizations and excuses.
5½ x 8½, 288 pp, Quality PB, 978-1-59473-310-9 **$16.99**

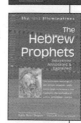

Tanya, the Masterpiece of Hasidic Wisdom
Selections Annotated & Explained
Translation & Annotation by Rabbi Rami Shapiro; Foreword by Rabbi Zalman M. Schachter-Shalomi
Clarifies one of the most powerful and potentially transformative books of Jewish wisdom. 5½ x 8½, 240 pp, Quality PB, 978-1-59473-275-1 **$18.99**

Zohar: Annotated & Explained
Translation & Annotation by Daniel C. Matt; Foreword by Andrew Harvey
The canonical text of Jewish mystical tradition.
5½ x 8½, 176 pp, Quality PB, 978-1-893361-51-5 **$18.99**

See Inspiration for *Perennial Wisdom for the Spiritually Independent: Sacred Teachings—Annotated & Explained*

Spiritual Practice—The Sacred Art of Living Series

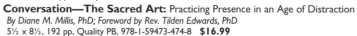

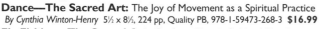

Dreaming—The Sacred Art: Incubating, Navigating & Interpreting Sacred Dreams for Spiritual & Personal Growth
By Lori Joan Swick
This fascinating introduction to sacred dreams celebrates the dream experience as a way to deepen spiritual awareness and as a source of self-healing. Designed for the novice and the experienced sacred dreamer of all faith traditions, or none.
5½ x 8½, 224 pp, Quality PB, 978-1-59473-544-8 **$16.99**

Conversation—The Sacred Art: Practicing Presence in an Age of Distraction
By Diane M. Millis, PhD; Foreword by Rev. Tilden Edwards, PhD
5½ x 8½, 192 pp, Quality PB, 978-1-59473-474-8 **$16.99**

Dance—The Sacred Art: The Joy of Movement as a Spiritual Practice
By Cynthia Winton-Henry 5½ x 8½, 224 pp, Quality PB, 978-1-59473-268-3 **$16.99**

Fly-Fishing—The Sacred Art: Casting a Fly as a Spiritual Practice
By Rabbi Eric Eisenkramer and Rev. Michael Attas, MD; Foreword by Chris Wood, CEO, Trout Unlimited; Preface by Lori Simon, executive director, Casting for Recovery
5½ x 8½, 160 pp, Quality PB, 978-1-59473-299-7 **$16.99**

Giving—The Sacred Art: Creating a Lifestyle of Generosity
By Lauren Tyler Wright 5½ x 8½, 208 pp, Quality PB, 978-1-59473-224-9 **$16.99**

Haiku—The Sacred Art: A Spiritual Practice in Three Lines
By Margaret D. McGee 5½ x 8½, 192 pp, Quality PB, 978-1-59473-269-0 **$16.99**

Hospitality—The Sacred Art: Discovering the Hidden Spiritual Power of Invitation and Welcome *By Rev. Nanette Sawyer; Foreword by Rev. Dirk Ficca*
5½ x 8½, 208 pp, Quality PB, 978-1-59473-228-7 **$16.99**

Labyrinths from the Outside In, 2nd Edition: Walking to Spiritual Insight—A Beginner's Guide *By Rev. Dr. Donna Schaper and Rev. Dr. Carole Ann Camp*
6 x 9, 208 pp, b/w illus. and photos, Quality PB, 978-1-59473-486-1 **$16.99**

Lectio Divina—**The Sacred Art**
Transforming Words & Images into Heart-Centered Prayer
By Christine Valters Paintner, PhD 5½ x 8½, 240 pp, Quality PB, 978-1-59473-300-0 **$16.99**

Pilgrimage—The Sacred Art: Journey to the Center of the Heart
By Dr. Sheryl A. Kujawa-Holbrook 5½ x 8½, 240 pp, Quality PB, 978-1-59473-472-4 **$16.99**

Practicing the Sacred Art of Listening: A Guide to Enrich Your Relationships and Kindle Your Spiritual Life *By Kay Lindahl* 8 x 8, 176 pp, Quality PB, 978-1-893361-85-0 **$18.99**

Recovery—The Sacred Art: The Twelve Steps as Spiritual Practice *by Rami Shapiro; Foreword by Joan Borysenko, PhD* 5½ x 8½, 240 pp, Quality PB, 978-1-59473-259-1 **$16.99**

Running—The Sacred Art: Preparing to Practice *By Dr. Warren A. Kay; Foreword by Kristin Armstrong* 5½ x 8½, 160 pp, Quality PB, 978-1-59473-227-0 **$16.99**

The Sacred Art of Chant: Preparing to Practice
By Ana Hernández 5½ x 8½, 192 pp, Quality PB, 978-1-59473-036-8 **$16.99**

The Sacred Art of Fasting: Preparing to Practice
By Thomas Ryan, CSP 5½ x 8½, 192 pp, Quality PB, 978-1-59473-078-8 **$15.99**

The Sacred Art of Forgiveness: Forgiving Ourselves and Others through God's Grace
By Marcia Ford 8 x 8, 176 pp, Quality PB, 978-1-59473-175-4 **$18.99**

The Sacred Art of Listening: Forty Reflections for Cultivating a Spiritual Practice
By Kay Lindahl; Illus. by Amy Schnapper 8 x 8, 160 pp, b/w illus., Quality PB, 978-1-893361-44-7 **$16.99**

The Sacred Art of Lovingkindness: Preparing to Practice
By Rabbi Rami Shapiro; Foreword by Marcia Ford 5½ x 8½, 176 pp, Quality PB, 978-1-59473-151-8 **$16.99**

Thanking & Blessing—The Sacred Art: Spiritual Vitality through Gratefulness
By Jay Marshall, PhD; Foreword by Philip Gulley 5½ x 8½, 176 pp, Quality PB, 978-1-59473-231-7 **$16.99**

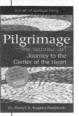

Writing—The Sacred Art: Beyond the Page to Spiritual Practice
By Rami Shapiro and Aaron Shapiro 5½ x 8½, 192 pp, Quality PB, 978-1-59473-372-7 **$16.99**

Social Justice

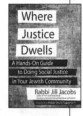

Where Justice Dwells
A Hands-On Guide to Doing Social Justice in Your Jewish Community
By Rabbi Jill Jacobs; Foreword by Rabbi David Saperstein
Provides ways to envision and act on your own ideals of social justice.
7 x 9, 288 pp, Quality PB Original, 978-1-58023-453-5 **$24.99**

There Shall Be No Needy
Pursuing Social Justice through Jewish Law and Tradition
By Rabbi Jill Jacobs; Foreword by Rabbi Elliot N. Dorff, PhD; Preface by Simon Greer
Confronts the most pressing issues of twenty-first-century America from a deeply Jewish perspective. 6 x 9, 288 pp, Quality PB, 978-1-58023-425-2 **$16.99**
There Shall Be No Needy Teacher's Guide 8½ x 11, 56 pp, PB, 978-1-58023-429-0 **$8.99**

Conscience
The Duty to Obey and the Duty to Disobey
By Rabbi Harold M. Schulweis
Examines the idea of conscience and the role conscience plays in our relationships to government, law, ethics, religion, human nature, God—and to each other.
6 x 9, 160 pp, Quality PB, 978-1-58023-419-1 **$16.99**; HC, 978-1-58023-375-0 **$19.99**

Judaism and Justice: The Jewish Passion to Repair the World
By Rabbi Sidney Schwarz; Foreword by Ruth Messinger
6 x 9, 352 pp, Quality PB, 978-1-58023-353-8 **$19.99**

Spirituality / Women's Interest

Embracing the Divine Feminine: Finding God through the Ecstasy of Physical Love—The Song of Songs Annotated & Explained
By Rabbi Rami Shapiro; Foreword by Rev. Cynthia Bourgeault, PhD
Restores the Song of Songs' eroticism and interprets it as a celebration of the love between the Divine Feminine and the contemporary spiritual seeker.
5½ x 8½, 176 pp, Quality PB, 978-1-59473-575-2 **$16.99**

The Quotable Jewish Woman
Wisdom, Inspiration & Humor from the Mind & Heart
Edited by Elaine Bernstein Partnow
6 x 9, 496 pp, Quality PB, 978-1-58023-236-4 **$19.99**

The Women's Haftarah Commentary
New Insights from Women Rabbis on the 54 Weekly Haftarah Portions, the 5 Megillot & Special Shabbatot
Edited by Rabbi Elyse Goldstein
Illuminates the historical significance of female portrayals in the Haftarah and the Five Megillot. 6 x 9, 560 pp, Quality PB, 978-1-58023-371-2 **$19.99**

The Women's Torah Commentary
New Insights from Women Rabbis on the 54 Weekly Torah Portions
Edited by Rabbi Elyse Goldstein
Over fifty women rabbis offer inspiring insights on the Torah, in a week-by-week format.
6 x 9, 496 pp, Quality PB, 978-1-58023-370-5 **$19.99**; HC, 978-1-58023-076-0 **$34.95**

The Divine Feminine in Biblical Wisdom Literature
Selections Annotated & Explained *Translation & Annotation by Rabbi Rami Shapiro*
Foreword by Rev. Cynthia Bourgeault, PhD
5½ x 8½, 240 pp, Quality PB, 978-1-59473-109-9 **$16.99***

New Jewish Feminism: Probing the Past, Forging the Future
Edited by Rabbi Elyse Goldstein; Foreword by Anita Diamant
6 x 9, 480 pp, HC, 978-1-58023-359-0 **$24.99**

*A book from SkyLight Paths, Jewish Lights' sister imprint

Women's Interest

She Lives! Sophia Wisdom Works in the World
By Rev. Jann Aldredge-Clanton, PhD
Fascinating narratives of clergy and laypeople who are changing the institutional church and society by restoring biblical female divine names and images to Christian theology, worship symbolism and liturgical language.
6 x 9, 320 pp, Quality PB, 978-1-59473-573-8 **$18.99**

Birthing God: Women's Experiences of the Divine
By Lana Dalberg; Foreword by Kathe Schaaf
Powerful narratives of suffering, love and hope that inspire both personal and collective transformation. 6 x 9, 304 pp, Quality PB, 978-1-59473-480-9 **$18.99**

Women, Spirituality and Transformative Leadership
Where Grace Meets Power
Edited by Kathe Schaaf, Kay Lindahl, Kathleen S. Hurty, PhD, and Reverend Guo Cheen
A dynamic conversation on the power of women's spiritual leadership and its emerging patterns of transformation.
6 x 9, 288 pp, Quality PB, 978-1-59473-548-6 **$18.99**; HC, 978-1-59473-313-0 **$24.99**

Spiritually Healthy Divorce: Navigating Disruption with Insight & Hope
By Carolyne Call A spiritual map to help you move through the twists and turns of divorce. 6 x 9, 224 pp, Quality PB, 978-1-59473-288-1 **$16.99**

New Feminist Christianity: Many Voices, Many Views
Edited by Mary E. Hunt and Diann L. Neu
Insights from ministers and theologians, activists and leaders, artists and liturgists offer a starting point for building new models of religious life and worship.
6 x 9, 384 pp, Quality PB, 978-1-59473-435-9 **$19.99**; HC, 978-1-59473-285-0 **$24.99**

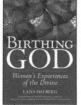

Bread, Body, Spirit: Finding the Sacred in Food
Edited and with Introductions by Alice Peck 6 x 9, 224 pp, Quality PB, 978-1-59473-242-3 **$19.99**

Dance—The Sacred Art: The Joy of Movement as a Spiritual Practice
By Cynthia Winton-Henry 5½ x 8½, 224 pp, Quality PB, 978-1-59473-268-3 **$16.99**

Daughters of the Desert: Stories of Remarkable Women from Christian, Jewish and Muslim Traditions
By Claire Rudolf Murphy, Meghan Nuttall Sayres, Mary Cronk Farrell, Sarah Conover and Betsy Wharton
5½ x 8½, 192 pp, Illus., Quality PB, 978-1-59473-106-8 **$14.99** Inc. reader's discussion guide

The Divine Feminine in Biblical Wisdom Literature
Selections Annotated & Explained
Translation & Annotation by Rabbi Rami Shapiro; Foreword by Rev. Cynthia Bourgeault, PhD
5½ x 8½, 240 pp, Quality PB, 978-1-59473-109-9 **$16.99**

Divining the Body: Reclaim the Holiness of Your Physical Self
By Jan Phillips 8 x 8, 256 pp, Quality PB, 978-1-59473-080-1 **$18.99**

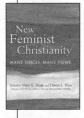

Honoring Motherhood: Prayers, Ceremonies & Blessings
Edited and with Introductions by Lynn L. Caruso
5 x 7¼, 272 pp, Quality PB, 978-1-58473-384-0 **$9.99**; HC, 978-1-59473-239-3 **$19.99**

Next to Godliness: Finding the Sacred in Housekeeping
Edited by Alice Peck 6 x 9, 224 pp, Quality PB, 978-1-59473-214-0 **$19.99**

The Triumph of Eve & Other Subversive Bible Tales
By Matt Biers-Ariel 5½ x 8½, 192 pp, Quality PB, 978-1-59473-176-1 **$14.99**

Woman Spirit Awakening in Nature: Growing Into the Fullness of Who You Are
By Nancy Barrett Chickerneo, PhD; Foreword by Eileen Fisher
8 x 8, 224 pp, b/w illus., Quality PB, 978-1-59473-250-8 **$16.99**

Women of Color Pray: Voices of Strength, Faith, Healing, Hope and Courage
Edited and with Introductions by Christal M. Jackson
5 x 7¼, 208 pp, Quality PB, 978-1-59473-077-1 **$15.99**

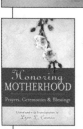

*A book from Jewish Lights, SkyLight Paths' sister imprint

About Jewish Lights

People of all faiths and backgrounds yearn for books that attract, engage, educate, and spiritually inspire.

Our principal goal is to stimulate thought and help all people learn about who the Jewish People are, where they come from, and what the future can be made to hold. While people of our diverse Jewish heritage are the primary audience, our books speak to people in the Christian world as well and will broaden their understanding of Judaism and the roots of their own faith.

We bring to you authors who are at the forefront of spiritual thought and experience. While each has something different to say, they all say it in a voice that you can hear.

Our books are designed to welcome you and then to engage, stimulate, and inspire. We judge our success not only by whether or not our books are beautiful and commercially successful, but by whether or not they make a difference in your life.

For your information and convenience, at the back of this book we have provided a list of other Jewish Lights books you might find interesting and useful. They cover all the categories of your life:

Bar/Bat Mitzvah	Life Cycle
Bible Study / Midrash	Meditation
Children's Books	Men's Interest
Congregation Resources	Parenting
Current Events / History	Prayer / Ritual / Sacred Practice
Ecology / Environment	Social Justice
Fiction: Mystery, Science Fiction	Spirituality
Grief / Healing	Theology / Philosophy
Holidays / Holy Days	Travel
Inspiration	Twelve Steps
Kabbalah / Mysticism / Enneagram	Women's Interest

Stuart M. Matlins, Publisher

Or phone, fax, mail or email to: **JEWISH LIGHTS Publishing**
Sunset Farm Offices, Route 4 • P.O. Box 237 • Woodstock, Vermont 05091
Tel: (802) 457-4000 • Fax: (802) 457-4004 • www.jewishlights.com
Credit card orders: (800) 962-4544 (8:30AM–5:30PM EST Monday–Friday)
Generous discounts on quantity orders. SATISFACTION GUARANTEED. Prices subject to change.

For more information about each book, visit our website at www.jewishlights.com

About SKYLIGHT PATHS Publishing

SkyLight Paths Publishing is creating a place where people of different spiritual traditions come together for challenge and inspiration, a place where we can help each other understand the mystery that lies at the heart of our existence.

Through spirituality, our religious beliefs are increasingly becoming a part of our lives—rather than *apart* from our lives. While many of us may be more interested than ever in spiritual growth, we may be less firmly planted in traditional religion. Yet, we do want to deepen our relationship to the sacred, to learn from our own as well as from other faith traditions, and to practice in new ways.

SkyLight Paths sees both believers and seekers as a community that increasingly transcends traditional boundaries of religion and denomination—people wanting to learn from each other, *walking together, finding the way.*

For your information and convenience, at the back of this book we have provided a list of other SkyLight Paths books you might find interesting and useful. They cover the following subjects:

Buddhism / Zen	Gnosticism	Poetry
Catholicism	Hinduism /	Prayer
Chaplaincy	Vedanta	Religious Etiquette
Children's Books	Inspiration	Retirement & Later-
Christianity	Islam / Sufism	Life Spirituality
Comparative	Judaism	Spiritual Biography
Religion	Meditation	Spiritual Direction
Earth-Based	Mindfulness	Spirituality
Spirituality	Monasticism	Women's Interest
Enneagram	Mysticism	Worship
Global Spiritual	Personal Growth	
Perspectives		

Or phone, fax, mail or email to: SKYLIGHT PATHS Publishing
Sunset Farm Offices, Route 4 • P.O. Box 237 • Woodstock, Vermont 05091
Tel: (802) 457-4000 • Fax: (802) 457-4004 • www.skylightpaths.com
Credit card orders: (800) 962-4544 (8:30AM–5:30PM EST Monday–Friday)
Generous discounts on quantity orders. SATISFACTION GUARANTEED. Prices subject to change.